CASE
FOR
MIRACLES
FOR KIDS

Other books in the Lee Strobel series for kids:

Case for Christ for Kids, Updated and Expanded
Case for a Creator for Kids, Updated and Expanded
Case for Faith for Kids, Updated and Expanded
Case for Grace for Kids
Case for Christ for Kids 90-Day Devotional

CASE
FOR
MIRACLES
FOR KIDS

LEE STROBEL

WITH JESSE FLOREA

ZONDERkidz

TABLE OF CONTENTS

"Miracles are a retelling in small letters of the very same story which is written across the whole world in letters too large for some of us to see."

–C. S. Lewis, Christian thinker and author of *The Chronicles of Narnia*[1]

"If miracles exist at all, they exist not for their own sake but for us, to point us toward something beyond. To Someone beyond."

–Eric Metaxas, journalist, speaker, and author of *Bible ABC*[2]

"Unless you people see signs and wonders, you will never believe."

–Jesus in John 4:48

"The most incredible thing about miracles is that they happen."

–G. K. Chesterton, novelist and Christian apologist[3]

INTRODUCTION

INVESTIGATING THE MIRACULOUS

Recently I was chatting with a former co-worker from my days as legal editor at the *Chicago Tribune* newspaper.

"You were the last person I ever thought would give up journalism to go tell people about Jesus," he said. "You were one of the most skeptical people

I knew. If I told you the deli down the block had a good sandwich, you wouldn't believe me until I produced a dozen restaurant reviews. Then I'd have to show you a certified chemical analysis of the ingredients from the Food and Drug Administration."

His comment made me laugh. And it's an obvious exaggeration. (I can judge a good sandwich just by taking a bite.) But, yes, my background in journalism and law did tend to make me a naturally doubtful person. And yet it was my doubt that ultimately led to my faith in Jesus.

When my wife, Leslie, started attending church and accepted Jesus Christ as her Savior, I wasn't happy. I wanted to prove to her that this newfound faith was wrong. I started to investigate the historical evidence of Christianity, just like I would investigate a news story.

To my dismay, the data of science (from cosmology and physics to biochemistry) convinced me there was a supernatural Creator. History told another compelling story. Jesus of Nazareth truly lived. He was crucified, buried, and resurrected from the dead—confirming his identity as the unique Son of God.

I concluded that Christianity was true. I couldn't ignore the evidence. And if it was true,

WORDS TO KNOW

Cosmology: the study of the beginning of the universe

Physics: the science that studies electricity, motion, sound, light, atoms, and the stars

Biochemistry: the science that studies chemical processes that happen in plant and animal cells

then I needed to change my life. I put my trust in Christ, left my newspaper career, and started using my life to tell others about Jesus.

However, my skeptical nature didn't just go away. Did I believe in miracles? Yes, of course . . . sort of. I was convinced that Jesus' resurrection and other miracles happened like the Bible said. But was God still in the miracle business today?

Some Christians believe that after the apostles died and the New Testament was compiled, signs and wonders stopped happening.[1]

Other followers of Christ point to Isaiah 53:5, which says, "By his wounds we are healed." They claim that if someone has enough faith in Jesus, physical healing can happen today. They see miracles all over the place.

MORE THAN 94 MILLION "MIRACLES"

As I began researching this book, I arranged for a national survey about miracles, which was done by Barna Research.[2] The survey found that half the adults in the United States (51 percent) said they believe the miracles of the Bible happened as they are described. Asked whether miracles are possible today, two out of three Americans (67 percent) said yes. Only 15 percent said no.

That was interesting. But what I really wanted to know was, how many people had personally experienced something they can only explain as being a miracle of God? Not surprisingly, Christians scored the highest percentage (nearly 78 percent) in reporting they had experienced God in a remarkable way.

But as it turned out, nearly two out of five U.S. adults (38 percent) said they have had such an experience. That means an eye-popping *94,792,000* Americans are convinced that God has performed at least one miracle for them.[3] That is an astonishing number!

Then I found a 2004 survey that showed 55

percent of U.S. doctors have seen results in their patients that they would consider miraculous.[4] Three quarters (75 percent) of the 1,100 doctors surveyed are convinced that miracles can happen today. That probably explains why six out of ten doctors said they pray for their patients individually.[5]

These statistics and surveys show people believe in miracles. But I wanted to dig deeper and still had a lot of questions. Maybe a lot of these supernatural occurrences were based on mistakes, misunderstandings, lies, legends, rumors, or wishful thinking.

In other words, does a miracle-performing God actually exist, and has he left his fingerprints all over history and into the present age? More importantly, is this same God available to perform supernatural events in *your* life today?

That's what I set out to determine in writing this book. While I'm a committed Christian whose convictions are widely known, I was truly interested in testing the strength of the case for miracles. I wanted to find the best experts and ask them hard questions. I wanted to investigate the science and find the truth.

I invite you to join me on this journey. When it comes to miracles, you need to tread carefully.

WORDS TO KNOW

Case: a legal term used to describe a set of facts and reasons that support an argument or belief

Some people make claims of miraculous healings in God's name when in reality they're only trying to gain riches and fame for themselves. So follow me as I follow the apostle Paul's words from 1 Thessalonians 5:20–22: "Don't be gullible. Check out everything, and keep only what's good. Throw out anything tainted with evil" (MSG). That's great advice! Before you truly believe something, you need to check it out. Look for the truth. Throw out the lies. Living this way can help you become wise . . . and help you find the facts about miracles. After all, if it's rational to believe in the miraculous, then the case surely should be able to stand up against challenges.

At the end of this book, I'll ask you to decide whether or not it does.

Questions About Miracles

1. What is your biggest question about miracles?

_____

_____

2. Have you ever experienced something that you'd call miraculous? Write down what happened.

_____

_____

_____

3. Put an X on the scale below to describe your current belief in miracles:

1	2	3	4	5	6	7	8	9	10

Don't think miracles happen   Totally think miracles happen

Why did you choose that number? What would it take for you to move higher on the scale?

_____

_____

CHAPTER 1

WHAT IS A MIRACLE?

Everyone had high hopes for Benjamin. He was the third-best student of his class in high school. Then he scored the highest SAT ranking of any student from a Detroit public school in twenty years.

He could only afford to pay the admission fee to apply to one college. He chose one of the top colleges in the country, Yale University in Connecticut. Fewer than one out of every twenty students who applies to Yale gets accepted. Ben not only got in, he was granted a full scholarship. He thought he was pretty hot stuff—until the end of his first semester.

Ben was failing chemistry, a prerequisite in fulfilling his dream of becoming a doctor. Everything depended on the final exam. But he wasn't ready for it, not by a long shot.

That evening, before the exam, he prayed. "Lord, medicine is the only thing I ever wanted to do. Would you please tell me what it is *you* really want me to do?"

He intended to study for the exam all night, but he fell asleep. It seemed that all was lost—until he had a dream. He was alone in an auditorium when a mysterious figure began writing chemistry problems on the blackboard.

"When I went to take the test the next morning, I recognized the first problem as one of the ones I had dreamed about," Ben says. "And the next, and the next, and the next. I aced the exam and got a good mark in chemistry. And I promised the Lord that he would never have to do that for me again."

Ben went on to achieve his goal of becoming a doctor. By age thirty-three, he became the youngest director of pediatric neurosurgery in the country. With his knowledge of how God designed the human body and his faith in Christ, Ben developed new types of operations at Johns Hopkins Hospital. He separated twins joined at the brain. He performed the first successful neurosurgery on a baby still in its mother's womb. He came up with new methods of treating brain stem and spinal cord tumors. And he was awarded the nation's highest civilian honor, the Presidential Medal of Freedom.

A 2014 poll ranked Benjamin Solomon Carson Sr. as among the ten most admired people in America. He even made a bid to become president of the United States. Although he didn't earn the nomination, he did earn a presidential cabinet position as the United States Secretary of Housing and Urban Development. And all of this happened because a dream helped him pass a chemistry course nearly fifty years prior.[1]

What do you think? Was this a coincidence? Or a miraculous intervention by God?

The word *miracle* gets thrown around a lot these days. I did a search on my computer for miracles and found all sorts of articles. Headlines popped up that read:

- "Boat Captain Rescues 'Miracle' Cat Thrown Off Bridge"
- "Miracle on Water Street: A Doctor Witnesses Crash, Saves Man's Life"
- "Miracle Baby Born the Size of a Tennis Ball Now Home"

A football player was said to need a "miracle" to find a team and continue his career. A diver who hit his head on the platform during a competition—and survived—was called a "miracle man."

All of these events certainly don't qualify as miracles. So what's the best way to define the miraculous? Philosophers and theologians have offered various descriptions. Personally, I like the definition offered by writer and professor Richard L. Purtill. He said a miracle had to meet certain conditions. So for an event to be a true miracle, it had to be:

1. brought about by the power of God
2. a temporary exception to the ordinary course of nature
3. for the purpose of showing that God acts in history[2]

To better understand this definition, imagine a

child with a heart condition. A doctor prescribes pills for the child and tells him, "When you start feeling pain in your chest, take a pill. If the pain continues, take another."

"What if I'm still hurting?" the child asks.

"You can take a third pill," the doctor says. "But if you do, make sure to immediately tell your parents and have them call an ambulance."

Not long after, the child wakes up with chest pains. He asks his mom for pill. He takes it, but it has no effect. A little later he takes another pill, but he is still in a lot of pain. His mom gives him a third pill and calls 911. The paramedics arrive and save his life.

Is that a miracle? Not really. The boy followed his doctor's orders and modern, lifesaving measures kept him alive.

But what if this same boy is riding his bike home from school and gets a flat tire? As he starts trying to fix his tire, he becomes unconscious and falls to the ground near a road. Two passing motorists stop. Both of them just happen to know CPR. One calls paramedics. The boy's heart is restarted and his life is spared once more.

Is that a miracle? Sure, God might have orchestrated it to have two people who knew CPR drive by. But Purtill would say, "There was nothing in the events to suggest any non-natural causes. The doctor's remarks, the training of the people who helped, the medical technology, are all things that seem to need no non-natural explanation."

Although Purtill would be grateful to God for the outcome (these *exact* things actually happened to him as an adult—except he was driving a car, not a bike), he doesn't consider it miraculous. He believes a lot of what people casually call "miracles" seem closer to fortunate "coincidences," or God at work through routine developments.

So how can you tell when something is a true miracle? For me, it comes down to seeing God's power displayed in an extraordinary way. Then there has to be additional sources or evidence that the event really happened as a person says. That's when the "miracle" bell goes off in my mind.

In other words, a dream about a mysterious figure writing chemistry problems on a blackboard isn't miraculous by itself. But if those equations are the very same problems that show up on a test the next day, that *does* seem miraculous, especially when the incident occurs after a prayer pleading for God's help.

So with that definition of a miracle in mind, let's go back to the miracle that started it all . . . the miracle of creation.

Questions About Miracles

1. This chapter begins with a story about an unusual dream that helped a young man achieve his lifelong goal. Does that seem like an actual miracle to you? Why?

_____

_____

_____

2. What kind of evidence would be necessary to convince you that a miracle has taken place?

_____

CHAPTER 2

THE MIRACLE
OF CREATION

Many Bible-believing scientists say the grand-daddy of all miracles is the creation of the universe from nothing. The first words in the Bible say, "In the beginning God created the heavens and the earth" (Genesis 1:1). If that statement is true, then "lesser" miracles become easier to believe. In other words, if God can command an entire universe to leap into existence, then walking on water would be like a stroll in the park. A resurrection would be as simple as the snap of his fingers.

Without a doubt, *creatio ex nihilo* (the Latin phrase for "creation out of nothing") is the most extraordinary miracle ever performed. God spoke. The universe was created. He designed the laws of nature. He made all the plants and animals. He formed human life.

But not everybody believes in creation. School textbooks and science teachers often explain the origins of life as happening by chance. They say the universe started with a big bang billions of years ago. Stars slowly formed. Planets began their orbits. Slowly, over millions and millions of years, the conditions on Earth allowed for single-celled organisms to grow. Life gradually became more complex until humans evolved from apes. God had nothing to do with it. It was a natural selection and chance. That's what science says, right?

Some scientists believe that. They look at the universe only through their scientific principles and don't have any room in their theories for God. They think, *The universe didn't have a cause. It just happened.* Or, *Perhaps there was no absolute beginning for everything.*

Other scientists study the universe and see a God-sized miracle. One such scientist is Michael G. Strauss.

WORDS TO KNOW

Theory: an idea based on testing and observation that explains an event or phenomenon

Strauss first became interested in science while growing up in Huntsville, Alabama. That's where NASA built the first stage of the mighty Saturn V rocket that took astronauts to the moon. There's still enthusiasm in his voice when he says, "They'd light those boosters to test them and—*wow!*—the whole town would shake!"

Strauss graduated as valedictorian of his high school class. He earned graduate and doctoral degrees from UCLA. To say he's smart is like saying atoms are small. It's an obvious fact to everybody. Strauss has been a physics professor for more than twenty years. He's spent much of that time studying and smashing together protons—some of the universe's tiniest particles—in massive collider labs.

Interestingly, Strauss's study of the world's tiniest particles has helped him understand the vastness and orderliness of the universe. When protons collide and explode into even tinier particles, scientists get a glimpse into the incredible complexity and wonder of God's creativity.

"The Bible says it's through the natural processes of nature that we most commonly see evidence for God, not just through his miracles," Strauss says. "Romans 1:20 tells us that God's invisible qualities are clearly seen—through what? Through what he has made.[1] And Psalm 19:1 says, 'The heavens declare the glory of God; the skies proclaim the work of his hands.' So, frankly, we don't necessarily need miracles to find evidence for God; it's right there, embedded in the natural processes that he has created and which we, as scientists, are studying."

IN THE BEGINNING

Scientists ask a lot of questions. A big part of their job is finding answers to those questions. As they study the universe, they ask, "Given what we observe, what has the highest probability? What has the most observational and experimental evidence to back it up?"

Anything is possible when it comes to the origins of the universe. But not everything is probable. Science shows that the universe is expanding and aging. Nearly every scientist agrees that the most probable conclusion from all the data is that the universe had a beginning. But the fact that the universe was created doesn't necessarily prove that God did it.

That's where Strauss and other scientists come in. They look at how the universe operates and see the fingerprints of an intelligent designer.

"And that's not only the opinion of Christian scientists," Strauss says. "Virtually every scientist agrees the universe is finely tuned—the question is: How did it get this way?[2] I think the most plausible explanation is that the universe was designed by a Creator."

Strauss can provide numerous complex, mind-boggling scientific examples that show how precisely the universe and Earth had to be created for intelligent life to exist. If everything didn't function like it does, life would be scientifically impossible.

One example is the amount of matter in the universe. As the universe expands, all matter is attracted to other matter by gravity. If there were too much matter, the universe would collapse on itself before stars and planets formed. If there were too little matter, stars and planets would never come together. But somehow the universe contains "just the right amount" of matter to sustain life.

Did this happen by accident? Or did a highly intelligent God know what he was doing?

Strauss's study of the atom offers another fine-tuning example from creation—the power of the *strong nuclear force*. This is the force that holds together the nucleus of an atom. It's the precise strength of this force that allows for the formation of all the elements on Earth. Many chemistry classrooms have a colorful periodic table of elements hanging on the wall. It displays all naturally occurring elements and their atomic numbers from one (hydrogen) to ninety-four (plutonium). Plus, there are several heavier elements that have only been created in laboratories or nuclear reactors.

"If you were to make the strong nuclear force just 2 percent stronger while all other constants stayed the same, you'd add a lot more elements to the periodic table, but they would be radioactive and life-destroying," Strauss says. "Plus, you'd have very little hydrogen in the universe."

Water is made from two hydrogen atoms and one atom of oxygen. So without enough hydrogen, there wouldn't be enough water. Since the human body is comprised of more than 60 percent water, that creates a problem.

"No water, no life," Strauss says matter-of-factly.

The opposite is also true. If the strong nuclear

force was decreased by a mere 5 percent, the only element in existence would be hydrogen. Again, a dead universe.

Strauss adds: "Not only is our universe precisely calibrated to a breathtaking degree, but our planet is also remarkably and fortuitously situated so life would be possible."

To have a planet like Earth where intelligent life exists, Strauss says many factors must be in place:

1. The right kind of galaxy. There are three types of galaxies: elliptical, spiral, and irregular. Life can only occur in a spiral galaxy, like our Milky Way. It's the only kind of galaxy that produces the right heavy elements and has the proper radiation levels.

2. The right location in the galaxy. If a planet is too close to the center, there's too much radiation. Not to mention black holes, which you want to avoid. But if a planet sits too far from the center, it would lack the oxygen and carbon needed for life.

3. The right kind of star. Our sun is a Class G star that supports stable planetary orbits. It is also a "bachelor" star. Many stars in the universe are binary, which means two stars

orbit each other. That's bad for stable planetary orbits. And without a stable orbit, a planet's temperatures could swing to life-killing extremes.

4. The right distance from the right star.

5. The right rotation rate. Not too fast and not too slow.

6. The right amount of water. Water is necessary for life, but too much can cause problems.

7. The right size so gravity lets gases, like methane, escape but allows oxygen to stay.

8. The right kind of moon. It's very rare for a planet to have just one large moon. The Earth's moon stabilizes our planet's tilt, which happens to be the perfect amount of tilt.

9. The right tectonic activity. The movement of the Earth's tectonic plates creates earthquakes. But experts say they're a key requirement for life on a planet.[3] Plate tectonics drive biodiversity, help create continents, and help generate Earth's magnetic field.

10. The right "blocker" planets close by. Planets such as Jupiter act like a vacuum cleaner by attracting potentially devastating comets and meteors into their gravitation field. When meteors hit Jupiter, it keeps them away from Earth.

WORDS TO KNOW

Astrophysicist: a scientist who studies stars, planets, and the universe

That may sound like a lot of conditions. But there are actually a lot more. Astrophysicist Hugh Ross says that three hundred and twenty-two conditions would have to be met to create an Earth-like planet.[4]

So, what are the chances that another Earth-like planet exists in the universe? Scientists ran the probability calculations. The results: there's a 10–304 chance of finding another planet that's truly like Earth.

That number is larger than a centillion, which is defined as the number one followed by 303 zeros. It's almost impossible to imagine a number that big. Of course, the universe is massive. Some scientists say there could be more than a billion trillion planets.

"So let's factor that number into our probability equation," Strauss says. "That still means the odds of having any higher life-supporting planet would be one in a million trillion trillion trillion trillion

trillion trillion trillion trillion trillion trillion trillion trillion trillion trillion trillion trillion trillion trillion trillion trillion trillion trillion trillion trillion."

Science has a phrase for those odds. Strauss explains: "It ain't gonna happen."

Christians also have a phrase for that kind of probability: It would take a miracle.

GOD VERSUS THE MULTIVERSE

With all the evidence pointing to the fact that the universe was designed, some scientists have created bizarre explanations for how this precision could have occurred in a purely naturalistic way, without an intelligent designer (God). One of these is the multiverse option.

An idea called M-theory allows for a near-infinite number of other universes. If all of these universes had a slightly different set of physics, sooner or later one universe would probably have the right conditions for life.

"Physicists have come up with various ideas for how multiverses could be birthed, but there's no observational or experimental evidence for it," Strauss says. "The theory may be untestable and non-falsifiable, and there's no observational evidence for it, so is it really science?"

In other words, if you want to believe in the

multiverse theory, you basically need blind faith.[5] Strangely enough, that's exactly the argument that scientists have used *against* the idea of God.

Maybe scientists should ask themselves what takes more faith: Believing in a comic book-like multiverse where life only exists because it hit the astronomical cosmic jackpot or believing that a loving God performed a miracle and created everything?

And if God is the most likely explanation for how our universe and planet began, then what can we learn about him from the scientific evidence?

Strauss thought of several things:

1. He must be transcendent, because he exists apart from his creation.
2. He must be timeless or eternal, since he existed before physical time.
3. He must be powerful.
4. He must be smart, given how masterfully the universe is finely tuned.
5. He must be personal, because he made the decision to create.
6. He must be creative.
7. He must be caring, because he so purposefully crafted Earth for us.

After looking at everything, I concluded the

God option has a pretty strong case. Creation *is* an amazing miracle.

Since God started everything with a miracle, my next step in building a case for miracles was to investigate if miracles still happen today. I know some scientists accept that a Creator made the universe, but they say that's *all* he did. They think he made everything and then sat back.

So did God set the planets spinning and then start relaxing? Or is this creative Designer still active and making his presence known in the world today? I was about to find out.

Questions About Miracles

1. Do you believe the universe was created by God? Why or why not?

_____

_____

_____

2. Romans 1:20 says, "For since the creation of the world God's invisible qualities—his eternal power and divine nature—have been clearly seen, being understood from what has been made, so that people are without excuse." Based on this verse, what aspects of nature point most strongly toward God's existence? Why?

_____

_____

_____

3. In addition to using the scientific method, what are some other ways we can determine whether something is true or not?

_____

_____

4. If God created the universe, then performing other miracles is mere child's play. Do you agree? Why or why not?

_____

_____

_____

5. This chapter explains several examples of our finely tuned universe and planet. How does this evidence point to the existence of God?

_____

_____

6. Scripture speaks to certain scientific truths. Look up the following verses and write down what they tell us about creation.

Colossians 1:15-17:

_____

_____

Jeremiah 10:12:

_____

_____

Jeremiah 33:25:

_____

_____

THE MIRACLE OF CREATION

Isaiah 45:12:

_____

_____

7.   The universe is so finely tuned that scientists
think this could have happened in only two ways:
a multiverse or a designer. In your view, which
explanation fits the evidence best?

_____

CHAPTER 3

A TIDE OF MIRACLES

In a country near the equator in Africa, a woman died in childbirth. She left behind a grieving two-year-old daughter and a premature baby in danger of dying during the chill of night. No hospitals were close by. With no incubator, no electricity, and few supplies, the newborn's life was in jeopardy.

A helper filled a hot water bottle to keep the baby warm. Suddenly, the rubber burst. The bottle was useless. And it was the last hot water bottle in the village.

A visiting missionary physician from Northern Ireland, Dr. Helen Roseveare, asked for prayer. A faith-filled ten-year-old orphan named Ruth spoke up, but she seemed to go too far.

"Please God, send us a water bottle," she prayed. "It'll be no good tomorrow, God. The baby will be dead. Please send it this afternoon." Then she added, "And while you are about it, would you please send a dolly for the little girl so she'll know you really love her?"

After the prayer, Roseveare remembers thinking, "Can I honestly say, 'Amen'? I just don't believe that God can do this. Oh, yes, I know that he can do everything. The Bible says so, but there are limits, aren't there?"

The only hope of getting a water bottle would be through the mail. But Roseveare had never received a package during the almost four years she had lived in Africa. "Anyway," she mused, "if anyone did send a parcel, who would put in a hot water bottle? I live on the equator!"

A couple of hours later, a car dropped off a twenty-two-pound package. The orphans helped open it and sort through the contents: some clothing for them, bandages for the leprosy patients, and a bit of food.

Oh, and this: "As I put my hand in again, I felt the . . . could it really be? I grasped it, and pulled it out. Yes. A brand-new rubber, hot water bottle!" Roseveare says. "I cried. I had not asked God to send it. I had not truly believed that he could."

With that, little Ruth rushed forward. "If God has sent the bottle, he must have sent the dolly too!" she exclaimed.

She dug through the packaging and found a beautifully dressed doll at the bottom of the box. Ruth looked up and said, "Can I go over with you, Mummy, and give this dolly to that little girl, so she'll know that Jesus really loves her?"

The arrival of the package couldn't have been more perfectly timed. Roseveare looked at the postmark. It had been packed *five months earlier* by her former Sunday school class. The leader had felt prompted by God to include a hot water bottle. A girl contributed the doll. And this package, the only one ever to arrive, was delivered the same day Ruth prayed for it.[1]

Is this a mere twist of fate? An embellished yarn? Or perhaps one of many modern-day miracles?

What's the longest book you've ever read?

One hundred pages? Three hundred? Many Bibles can be more than one thousand pages long.

Dr. Craig Keener doesn't just read long books. He writes them. As a professor of biblical studies, he spent years studying the book of Acts in the New Testament. Then he wrote a book about Acts that was nearly four thousand five hundred pages! Actually, it filled four books, because all those pages couldn't fit in one volume.

During his research, Keener was amazed at how many miracles occurred in the early church. He wanted to show that the history recorded in Acts was true. Because of all the stories of miracles in Acts, some people dismissed the book as tall tales. Keener felt if he could find accurate, provable modern-day miracles, then it was reasonable to believe that similar events happened thousands of years ago.

The more he researched miracles, the more convinced he became that miracles are more common than a lot of people think. And not just stories *about* miracles. Keener discovered documented miracles with lots of witnesses. He traveled to Africa to investigate seemingly supernatural healings. The deeper he dug, the more examples he found of modern wonders, marvels, visions, and dreams.

"Everywhere I looked, I came across miracle claims that better fit a supernatural explanation than a naturalistic conclusion," Keener says. "Pretty soon, there was a tidal wave of examples."

Two years later, his book *Miracles* was published. It filled two volumes and a staggering 1,172 pages!

The book spilled over with amazing stories of paralytics suddenly able to walk. Broken bones instantly mended. Hearing for the deaf. Sight for the blind. Burns disappearing. And many, many more modern-day miracles that occurred right after prayers to Jesus.

The stories came from around the world—China, Mozambique, the Philippines, Nigeria, Argentina, Brazil, Cuba, Ecuador, Indonesia, South Korea, and other countries. Multiple and independent eyewitnesses with reputations for integrity, including doctors, confirmed these miracles. In many cases, names, dates, and medical documentation proved the healings. There was even a scientific study confirming the healing of the deaf.

A DEAF CHILD HEARS

In September 1982, a nine-year-old British girl was diagnosed with deafness after a virus severely damaged the nerves in both of her ears.

"Her case is reported by Dr. R. F. R. Gardner, a well-credentialed physician,"[2] Keener says. "What makes this case especially interesting is that there is medical confirmation before the healing and immediately afterward."

The child's medical record says she was diagnosed with "untreatable bilateral sensorineural deafness." In other words, the tiny hairs in her inner ear had been damaged beyond repair. The girl's doctor told her parents that there was no cure. She was outfitted with hearing aids that helped her hear a little.

The girl didn't want to wear hearing aids the rest of her life. She started to pray that God would heal her. Her family and friends joined her. In fact, her mother felt prompted to pray specifically for healing.

Six months after being declared deaf, the girl went to an audiologist (a doctor that specializes in hearing) because one of her hearing aids had been damaged at school. After being examined and refitted, she was sent home.

The next day—March 9, 1983—the child suddenly jumped out of her bed without her hearing aids and came bounding down the stairs. "Mummy, I can hear!" she exclaimed.

Her mother tested to see if her daughter could detect noises and words. She could even hear whispers! Her mother excitedly called the audiologist.

"I don't believe you," the audiologist said. "It is not possible."

The audiologist asked for the girl to be tested again on the following day. When she went into the office, her hearing was fully restored.

"I can give no explanation for this," said the audiologist. "I have never seen anything like it in my life."

The girl's doctor ruled out possible medical explanations. In the medical report, the child's Ear, Nose, and Throat surgeon used the word "inexplicable" to describe what happened. He wrote, "An audiogram did show her hearing in both ears to be totally and completely normal. I was completely unable to explain this phenomenon but naturally, like her parents, I was absolutely delighted . . . I can think of no rational explanation as to why her hearing returned to normal."[3]

"A TIDE OF MIRACLES"

Keener could talk for hours about the cases he found in his search for miraculous claims. For example, he has three hundred and fifty reports of people who have been healed of blindness. Here are a few more true stories from his book:

- A welder named David Dominong suffered extensive third- and fourth-degree burns when he was electrocuted, in October 2002.

He was hospitalized for more than five weeks, and told it could be five years until he would be able to walk again. He was confined to a wheelchair and considering amputation until he went to a church, where the pastor prayed over him and he was promptly able to walk and run without assistance.

- Matthew Dawson was hospitalized in Australia with confirmed meningitis in April 2007. He was told he would have to remain under hospital care for weeks or months. But he was abruptly healed at the exact moment his father, on another continent, offered prayers for him.

- Mirtha Venero Boza, a medical doctor in Cuba, reported that her baby granddaughter's hand was severely burned by a hot iron, resulting in swelling and skin peeling off. Less than half an hour after prayer, however, the hand was completely healed without medical treatment. It looked like it had never been burned.

- Joy Wahnefried, a student at Taylor University in Indiana, suffered from an eye condition that gave her debilitating migraine headaches that could last up to a week. A professor and students prayed for her during three consecutive prayer meetings. Joy was suddenly healed. Her eyesight became perfect, and her incurable medical condition disappeared. Her eye doctor said she "can't explain it" and had never seen anything like it in the four thousand patients she had cared for.

Keener can retell so many miracles that after a while it's easy to become numb to them. While some of these stories come from the United States, many are from countries that don't have a lot of medical technology. Keener points out that God often uses miracles today like he did in the early church—to show his power and spread his truth.

Some experts estimate that 90 percent of the growth of the Christian church in China is being fueled by healings. This is especially true in the countryside, where medical facilities are often inadequate or nonexistent.[4]

Since about the mid-1980s, researchers have studied a tide of miracles that has begun to engulf the entire planet.[5] A Baptist church in India grew from six members to more than six hundred in just over a year because of healings. In Brazil, many poor people lack adequate health care. They're attracted to Christianity when they see healings and experience God's love.

After following all the evidence and looking into past and current reports about miracles, Keener came to one conclusion: "It looks like God is still in the miracle business! In light of the millions of people around the globe who say they've experienced the miraculous, it's time to take these claims seriously."

And since God interacts with his creation today, it's important to look back at the ultimate divine intervention—when God sent his Son to Earth. The miracle of Jesus' birth, death, and resurrection is the next step in building a case for miracles.

Questions About Miracles

1. Why do you think Dr. Helen Roseveare was uncomfortable with Ruth's prayer? What do you think Ruth thought when the water bottle showed up?

_____

_____

2. From researching his book, Craig Keener found hundreds of reports of miracles, including the healing of a broken ankle, deafness, and a heart condition. What's your response to these reports?

_____

_____

3. Miraculous healings are fueling the growth of Christian churches around the world, including in China, the Philippines, Brazil, and Ethiopia. Why do you think God is using his power in such a dramatic way in these places?

_____

_____

CHAPTER 4

MIRACLES OF JESUS

Winds rip at Tyler Armstrong's tent, gusting to fifty miles per hour. The nylon fabric shudders and rumbles in the wind, making it impossible to sleep. But nobody on Tyler's climbing team is sleeping at three a.m. With temperatures at negative nineteen degrees Fahrenheit, everybody is already awake. The camp is alive with activity as the team prepares to summit Mount Aconcagua in Argentina.

But there's a problem, and it's not the freezing temperatures. It's the wind. At just nine years old, Tyler doesn't weigh enough to safely climb in winds above thirty-five miles per hour. And safety is the main issue when you're trying to conquer one of the world's tallest mountains.

Every year people die trying to summit Aconcagua. Known as the "Colossus of America," it stands at 22,834 feet—the tallest mountain in the southern hemisphere. Aconcagua is the highest peak outside of Asia and the second tallest mountain of the Seven Summits, which are the highest points on each continent. Only Mount Everest, at 29,035 feet, is taller.

Tyler and his team have already made it to 19,200 feet above sea level. They have less than four thousand vertical feet to climb to make it to the top. But the last bit of the journey is steep and dangerous. The team has been climbing for nearly two weeks. Supplies are low and bad weather is coming in. There's only a narrow window of opportunity to make it to the top.

So as the storm blasts the mountain, Tyler has a decision to make: press on or go back. Tyler's dad leaves the decision to his son. He's trained Tyler to be brave and smart.

Tyler has already shown a lot of bravery on the

expedition. Before the climb even started, he had to appear before an Argentinian court without his parents and ask for a special waiver that would allow him to climb Aconcagua. No one under fourteen years old is normally allowed on the slippery slopes. The judge was impressed with Tyler's maturity and mountaineering experience, so he gave the young man permission.

Now the nine-year-old must show his smarts.

"Those who know when to turn around are the ones who survive," Tyler says. "Those who press forward when safety is questionable don't always make it back. The mountain will always be there."

At 3:30 in the morning, Tyler and his dad gather the team to pray. They ask God for wisdom and for the winds to stop. Storms here can last days, even weeks. If the weather doesn't improve in the next thirty minutes, they'll have no choice but to head down the mountain, wasting eighteen months of training, weeks of climbing, and thousands of dollars.

Tyler tells everybody it's too dangerous to continue. The team is disappointed, but they have a peace about the decision. They knew going into the journey that only about half of the most experienced climbers ever make it to the top.

Then God changes things. Only a few minutes

after Tyler's team prays together, the wind stops. The weather begins to clear, and the day is nearly perfect. God has given Tyler the green light.

The team quickly finishes getting ready. They put on their boots, zip up their jackets, and slip on their backpacks. Hours later, on December 24, 2013, Tyler sets the world record as the youngest person to ever summit Aconcagua!

Tyler will always remember that day as the Miracle on the Mountain.[1] But what do you think? Was this a weird weather anomaly? A trumped-up news story? Or maybe it's another example of Jesus calming the storm?

The Bible records about three dozen miracles performed by Jesus of Nazareth.

He controlled the weather, healed the blind, walked on water, multiplied food, raised the dead, and performed numerous other wonders. The gospel of John says what's mentioned is just a sampling of all the miracles Jesus did.[2]

If you just flip your Bible open to any place in the Gospels, you're bound to read about a miracle. Jesus' very life was bookended by two miracles that display God's amazing power—his birth by the virgin Mary and his resurrection after dying on the cross.

But can the Gospel writers be trusted? Sure, these books contain a lot of stories about miracles, but what if these writers got together and made up everything they wrote?

To get to the truth, I turned to former police detective J. Warner Wallace. Wallace had used his considerable crime-fighting skills to work for the Los Angeles sheriff's department, the SWAT team, and eventually the cold-case homicide unit. He solved murders that were previously unsolvable—some of which were decades old. For Wallace, facts needed to be solid, witnesses had to be credible, evidence must be persuasive, and corroboration was crucial. In short, he was the kind of skeptic I could relate to.

Not only was Wallace a solver of crimes, he was also an investigator of the Bible. Before he became a Christian, he spent months examining the Gospels. He used various investigative techniques, including what detectives call "forensic statement analysis." This skill involves critically analyzing a person's account of events—including word choice and structure—to determine whether he is being truthful or deceptive.[3]

His investigation ended up convincing him that the Gospels reliably recorded true events. Jesus was the Son of God. He performed miracles. He also died, was buried, and rose from the grave.

Wallace became convinced that Christianity is true beyond a reasonable doubt, and he committed his life to serving God.

THE EYEWITNESS GOSPELS

As Wallace studied the Gospels, he found strong evidence that John and Matthew wrote what they saw and heard as disciples of Jesus. They walked and talked with Jesus during his three years of ministry on earth. Luke wasn't a witness himself, but he said he "carefully investigated everything from the beginning."[4] And historical sources confirm that Mark was a scribe for the apostle Peter.

Wallace tested the Gospels like he would any eyewitness testimony.

"All eyewitness accounts have to be tested for reliability," Wallace says. "We can apply these tests to the Gospels—for instance, is there any corroboration, did the witnesses have a motive to lie,

WORDS TO KNOW

Scribe: a person who carefully writes down an official record of events did their stories change over time? When we do, we find they hold up well."

The Gospels were written to make moral points, teach us about Jesus, and help us know how to live. But that doesn't mean they don't report on real historical happenings. In fact, the Gospels are widely viewed by scholars as being biographies.[5]

Wallace not only studied the Gospels, he also created a timeline for some of the New Testament books. Luke's gospel was written before Acts, which was also written by Luke. Acts doesn't report several major events that occurred during the decade of AD 60, including Paul, Peter, and James being killed for their faith in Jesus. Experts believe that's because Acts was written before those early followers of Christ died. And we know Mark was written before Luke, because Luke uses Mark as one of his sources. Even before that, Paul confirms the resurrection in material that goes back to within months of Jesus' crucifixion.[6]

That means Mark was written less than thirty years after Jesus died. Thirty years may sound like a long time. But think about this: The Gospels were written during the lifetime of people who saw and followed Jesus—both his friends and his enemies. If any of the stories were made up or changed, surely someone would have disputed the facts and forced the accounts to be corrected. Plus, the Gospels were passed along verbally before being written down. In Wallace's mind, this helps the case for the accuracy of the Gospels.

Wallace has seen witnesses in his murder investigations recall thirty-five-year-old memories like they happened yesterday. After all those years, the details remain still crystal clear. Why? Because not all memories are created the same.

"If you asked me what I did on Valentine's Day five years ago, I probably couldn't recall very much," Wallace explains. "But if you asked me what I did on Valentine's Day forty years ago, I can give you a detailed report of what took place . . . because that's the day I got married."

When witnesses experience something that's unique, unrepeated, and personally important or powerful, they're much more likely to remember it. Many of the disciples' experiences with Jesus fit that description. Seeing Jesus walk on water would stick with you. Watching him lift a lame man to his feet or make a blind man see would be very memorable events.

Could they remember all the times their boat got stuck in a storm? Probably not. But could they remember the time Jesus commanded a storm to stop? Definitely.

Nearly 40 percent of the gospel of Mark involves miracles in some way.

And when you think of the resurrection, it was assuredly the most unique, unrepeated, and powerful thing any of the disciples had experienced. To see the risen Lord, scars on his hands and love in his eyes, would be something they would remember forever with vivid clarity.

DEALING WITH GOSPEL DIFFERENCES

But some people argue the Gospels can't be accurate because their accounts of the same event aren't identical. For instance, Matthew, Mark, and Luke all say multiple women visited Jesus' tomb and discovered it was empty. The stories don't, however, agree on the number of women. Depending on the gospel, it was two (Matthew) or more than three (Luke). John's gospel only mentions Mary Magdalene. So who was right? Or does this discrepancy show that the gospels are filled with errors?

Wallace says the differences actually prove the Bible's accuracy and honesty.

"Based on my years as a detective, I would expect the four gospels to have variances," Wallace says. "Think of this: the early believers could have destroyed all but one of the gospels in order to eliminate any differences between them. But they didn't. Why? Because they knew the gospels were true and that they told the story from different perspectives, emphasizing different things."

In Wallace's experience as a detective, eyewitness accounts of the same event often included discrepancies. Different details stood out to different people. They saw things in different ways. So the fact that the Gospels don't tell each story of Jesus' life in exactly the same way shows that the writers were telling the truth.

"Besides," Wallace adds, "if they meshed too perfectly, it would be evidence of collusion. The differences between the gospels actually show their cohesion in a way that would be expected if they were based on independent eyewitness accounts."

The Gospels also fill in the gaps for each other. In the book of Matthew, it says that during Jesus' trial, the chief priests and members of the council

WORDS TO KNOW

Collusion: a secret plan between people to falsify facts

struck him and said, "Prophesy to us, Messiah. Who hit you?"[7]

It seems like that would be pretty obvious, right? Couldn't Jesus just look at his attackers and identify them? But when Luke describes the same scene, he mentions one other detail: Jesus was blindfolded.

"Mystery solved," Wallace says. "By reporting what they saw, the gospel writers unintentionally included these unplanned supporting details."

Not only do the Gospels fill in the gaps for each other, archaeological evidence has been dug up that verifies certain points of Jesus' life. There are also non-Christian accounts outside the Bible that back up key gospel claims. Numerous ancient manuscripts help confirm what the original gospels said.

After all his research, tests, and studies, Wallace came to a conclusion: "The Gospels can be messy—just like you'd expect from a collection of eyewitness accounts. So I became convinced that they constitute reliable testimony to the life, teachings, death, and—yes, the resurrection—of Jesus."

DID JESUS REALLY DIE AND RISE AGAIN?

Ah, the resurrection.

Opponents of Christianity are constantly coming up with different ideas that try to cast doubt on whether Jesus died and rose from the grave. Some of these theories say Jesus never died on the cross or that Jesus' followers substituted somebody else in Jesus' place. Basically, they want to explain what happened *without* admitting that it took a miracle like the resurrection.

To combat these arguments, Christians need to prove two things:

1. Jesus actually died from crucifixion.
2. Jesus was encountered alive after the empty tomb was discovered.

The first point is the easiest to prove. The Gospels describe Jesus' brutal journey to the cross. Pontius Pilate had Jesus beaten to within an inch of his life. His flogging was horrific. Jesus was in such bad shape that he couldn't even carry his cross all the way to Golgotha, the place where he would be crucified. He started carrying it (John 19:17), but along the way Jesus became too weak and Simon the Cyrene carried the cross the rest of the way (Mark 15:21). Because of the severity of his injuries, the Bible says Jesus died well before the thieves who were crucified with him.

"The objection that Jesus wasn't really dead usually comes from people who have never been around dead bodies," Wallace says. "As a cop, let me tell you: dead people aren't like corpses in movies. They look different. They feel different. The Roman soldiers knew what death looked like. In fact, they were motivated to make sure Jesus was deceased, because they would be executed if a prisoner escaped alive."

In other words, the Romans didn't make mistakes when it came to death. They were masters at punishing criminals and carrying out their orders. When the soldiers took Jesus away from Pilate and led him to the cross, it *was* Jesus who died. There was no mistake, no substitution, and no doubt.

In fact, Wallace pointed out, scholars have looked at all the literature on Jesus' resurrection going back thirty years, and his death was among the facts that were almost unanimously accepted.[8]

"Besides, we have no record of anyone ever surviving a full Roman crucifixion," Wallace adds. "And the apostle John gave us a major clue that Jesus was really dead."

John wrote that when one of the soldiers stabbed Jesus' side with a spear, water and blood came out.[9] In those days, nobody understood what that meant, medically. Today, doctors know this would be expected, because the beatings would have caused fluid to collect around Jesus' heart and lungs. Without even realizing it, John provides a detail that helps prove Jesus was dead.

Then there's the second point—that people saw and talked to a physical Jesus after his death. The Bible provides plenty of evidence for the risen Christ.

Jesus appeared to Mary Magdalene at the empty tomb. And he famously appeared to Thomas and the other disciples, asking Thomas if he wanted to put his hand in the wounds on Jesus' hands and side. Only a physical Jesus would have the scars for Thomas to touch.[10]

Jesus appeared to others, even to large groups of people. He also caught and cooked fish for his disciples when they returned from a fishing trip—something only a physical person could do.[11]

That's some strong evidence. But Wallace says the disciples' actions and behavior regarding the resurrection are the strongest support for the truth of Jesus rising from the dead. At least seven ancient sources tell us the disciples were willing to suffer and die for their belief that they encountered the risen Jesus.[12] Even more importantly, there isn't a single ancient document or claim in which any of the eyewitnesses ever changed or denied their testimony.

"What's important is their *willingness* to die,"

Wallace says. "They knew the truth about what occurred. My experience is that people aren't willing to suffer or die for what they know is a lie."

Over and over, to this day, followers of Christ are willing to risk their lives and die for their belief in the resurrected Jesus. His miracle of rising from the dead for the forgiveness of sins creates the opportunity of a personal miracle for his followers through redemption and new life. That's the enduring power of the miracle of the resurrection. And it's a miracle Jesus wants shared with others.

Think about his last words to the disciples: "Then Jesus came to them and said, 'All authority in heaven and on earth has been given to me. Therefore go and make disciples of all nations, baptizing them in the name of the Father and of the Son and of the Holy Spirit, and teaching them to obey everything I have commanded you. And surely I am with you always, to the very end of the age'" (Matthew 28:18–20).

Jesus wants other people to know about his miracles, especially about the new life people can experience through him. He wants his miracles—both in the past and today—to be looked at and studied.

So that was my next step . . . to examine the science of miracles.

Questions About Miracles

1. Do you believe the miracles of Jesus occurred as described in the New Testament gospels (Matthew, Mark, Luke, and John)? Which of Jesus' supernatural acts is your favorite? Please explain.

_____

_____

_____

2. J. Warner Wallace said that when witnesses experience something that's unique, unrepeated, and personally important or powerful, they are much more likely to remember it. Can you think of an example of this from your own life? How does this help you believe more in the truthfulness of the Gospels?

_____

_____

_____

3. If the Gospels are true and Jesus died for our sins and rose from the dead, then it's the most important event in history. Have you shared your faith in Jesus with anybody before? If so, what happened? If not, what's stopping you?

_____

_____

_____

4. Write down the names of two people you want to tell about Jesus' miracle of the resurrection and the miracle of what he did in your life.

_____

_____

CHAPTER 5

THE SCIENCE OF MIRACLES

Angela couldn't believe she'd finally made it to Australia. She'd heard about how beautiful the country was from her mother and grandfather, but words couldn't properly describe it. She planned to spend the next eight months in the Land Down Under, completing discipleship training school in Brisbane with Youth With A Mission (YWAM).

Just two weeks into her training in 2005, she and the other students were taken into the outback for a team-building weekend. At twenty-three years old, Angela was one of the oldest students. But at camp, she immediately connected with other Christian kids from around the world. The weekend flew by, and Angela didn't want it to end. Then she learned it didn't have to—one of the YWAM leaders offered to lead a group up a nearby mountain into the Australian rainforest.

She jumped at the chance. So did a lot of the students. In the end, two vans full of adventurers drove to the base of the mountain and began the hike.

The Australian rainforest was hot and humid—and one of the most amazing places she had ever seen. Vines hung from giant trees. Colorful flowers bloomed. Birds and insects chattered.

Nervously, Angela grabbed a vine and jumped. "Whoo!" she shouted, swinging past her new friends. Soon the entire group was climbing up and swinging from vines as they steadily worked their way up the mountain.

All around her, the views were spectacular. She even saw a huge Australian eagle. By the time they reached the summit, beautiful pinks and purples sprinkled the golden sunset.

That's when it hit everybody: they still had to walk more than three miles back to the vans, and no one had a flashlight!

The leaders immediately got the group started back down the mountain. The sun glowed orange through the leaves, but it was quickly getting dark. Everybody broke into a run. Angela carefully watched her footing, trying not to trip over roots and rocks. Running was dangerous, but getting trapped in the rainforest at night was worse. Australia may be beautiful, but it's also home to poisonous plants, deadly snakes, ghost bats, leeches, sink holes, and other perils.

Finally, it was too dark to run. The thick covering of trees above didn't let in any light. No shining stars. No glowing moon. Even with her eyes open, Angela could barely see her hand in front of her face. One of the leaders had a flip phone that gave off a little light. He went up front and told everybody to hold hands and form a human chain. As they carefully plodded their way down the path, another leader had an idea.

"We should pray," he said.

The group immediately formed a circle and held hands.

"God, please light our path," one person prayed.

"Lord," another person chimed in, "in your Word, it talks about little balls of light. God, send us little balls of light."

Angela opened her eyes. *Yes, God, please light*

our path, she thought. Then she saw it . . . well, actually, she saw *them*.

Fireflies appeared everywhere! She hadn't seen these glowing bugs since she was a little girl. Now hundreds of fireflies surrounded the group. Their flickering, glimmering light chased away the darkness.

Angela looked around, amazed at the immediate answer to prayer.

"Let's keep walking," one the leaders said. "I can see the way again."

As they hiked down the trail, the fireflies flew right next to them. Now, instead of a scary place, the rainforest was beautiful again.

Miles later, when the canopy of trees finally broke, the group burst into celebration—jumping, laughing, praising God, and hugging. Angela looked to the sky with tears in her eyes, knowing that God had heard their prayers. Her faith in God was strong before, but now she felt like she could move a mountain!

Then, as suddenly as the fireflies had appeared, they disappeared back into the rainforest.[1]

Do you think this was some sort of strange insect infestation? An easily explained scientific phenomena? Or could it have been God nudging his creation to help some of his followers stay safe?

Miracles can't be analyzed in a test tube or studied under a microscope. Still, there are ways that science and medicine can contribute to the investigation of the supernatural. Test tubes can be used to check if a virus has suddenly disappeared from the blood of a sick patient immediately after prayer. An audiometer can be used to measure if a deaf person's hearing has been restored. In other words, science and faith, working side by side, can bring new understandings about our life and world.

Certainly, the use of scientific expertise can determine whether claims of the miraculous are valid or not. Even if science cannot definitively prove that something supernatural has occurred, it can provide empirical evidence that either supports or undermines accounts of miracles.

As Christians, we shouldn't fear or dismiss science. After all, Jesus was open to having his own miracles scrutinized. He told eyewitnesses to his miracles to report what they had seen.[2] He instructed a person healed of leprosy to show himself to the priest so he could be examined.[3]

So what is the legitimate role of science in investigating supernatural claims? To find the answer to that question, I turned to Indiana University

WORDS TO KNOW

Empirically: based on experiment, observation, and experience

professor Candy Gunther Brown. This Harvard-educated scholar focuses on how people's religious beliefs have real-world effects that can be studied empirically.[4] She's traveled the world to investigate how prayer can lead to supernatural healing, and she's written several books on the subject.

As she looks at the effects of prayer, Brown doesn't go in with a predetermined conclusion. She just follows where the facts point.

"Let's face it: people get sick, and when they do, they often pray for healing," Brown says. "Whether scientists or medical doctors think this is a good idea or not, it's going to happen. So it only makes sense to find out what occurs when there are prayers for healing. Are they beneficial, whether for natural or supernatural reasons? Or do they cause people to get worse?"

Brown compares medical records before and after prayer occurs. She checks to see if X-rays, blood tests, or other diagnostic reports showed illness or injury. Then she studies to see if there's been some resolution of that condition. Even with this evidence, she can't conclusively prove God healed a person, even if his or her illness disappears.

Brown says there are a lot of variables:

1. A person's medical treatment may have suddenly worked.
2. A patient may experience the placebo effect and think he's getting better.
3. Cases of spontaneous remission, where the body's immune system fights off the disease or the disease simply disappears.

But Brown says if there's no improvement or a worsening of their illness, we can say prayer for a miracle cure definitely *didn't* work. "Science is better at disproving things than proving them," she notes.

WORDS TO KNOW

Placebo effect: when the belief in a pill, treatment, or activity makes a person feel better, even though there is no proven medical benefit or actual medicine

THE EFFECTS OF PRAYER

Studies on the effects of prayer have been done for decades. In a study published in 1988, Dr. Randolph Byrd looked at two groups of patients. For one group, Christians were given the patient's first name, condition, and diagnosis. They were instructed to pray to God for a rapid recovery and for God to prevent medical complications and death. They could also pray for other areas in the patient's life that they believed to be beneficial. The other group of patients didn't receive any direct prayer.

The results?

Patients in the prayer group had less congestive heart failure, fewer heart attacks, fewer cases of pneumonia, were able to breathe better without the help of machines, and needed less medicine.

Then a decade or so later, a similar study was done by a team led by Dr. William S. Harris. They looked at the effects of prayer on almost a thousand patients in a hospital where patients had heart problems. Half received prayer; the other half didn't. Again, the group that received prayer had better outcomes.

DISTANT VERSUS PERSONAL PRAYER

While these studies showed that prayer could have a powerful impact, they didn't reflect the way prayers for healing were done in the Bible. The studies conducted by Drs. Byrd and Harris focused on *distant prayer*. The people praying were given the first name and condition of someone they didn't know and were told to pray for a complication-free surgery and quick recovery.

As you read about the healings performed by Jesus and the other disciples, they generally followed a totally different pattern. When they prayed, they often came within *close* physical contact with the person in need of healing. The hurting person knew they were being prayed for. They could feel the empathy, love, and caring of the prayers.

Jesus often touched those he was about to heal. For instance, Luke 4:40 says, "At sunset, the people brought to Jesus all who had various kinds of sickness, and laying his hands on each one, he healed them." What's more, the Bible says that the ill should be anointed with oil, which usually involves being touched on the head.[5]

To study the effects of up-close-and-personal prayer, Brown and her team flew to Mozambique. Located on the southeast coast of Africa, this desperately poor nation of twenty-five million people underwent a devastating civil war from 1977 to 1992. Almost half of the country is Christian, eighteen percent are Muslims, some believe in spirits that live in trees and other parts of nature, and the rest don't claim any religion.[6]

Brown focused on the healing of those with severe vision or hearing problems—some of whom were legally blind or deaf. Her team used standard tests and technical equipment to determine the person's level of hearing or vision loss immediately before prayer from a local missionary. After the prayers were concluded, the patient was promptly tested again. The length of the prayer varied, from one minute to five or ten minutes, but it always involved appropriate physical touch.

"After the missionaries prayed, we found highly significant improvements in hearing and statistically significant improvements in vision," Brown says. "We saw improvement in almost every single person we tested. Some of the results were quite dramatic."

In all, twenty-four people received prayer. One woman couldn't see her hand in front of her face. But once the missionary put her arms around the woman, hugged her, and prayed for one minute, the woman could see well enough to read.

An elderly blind and deaf woman named Martine had no response at 100 decibels in either ear, which meant she couldn't hear a jackhammer if it were being used next to her. After prayer, she responded at 75 decibels in her right ear and 40 decibels in her left ear, which meant she could now hear regular conversations. After a second prayer, Martine's eyesight improved from 20/400 to 20/80 on the vision chart. This meant she went from being legally blind to seeing objects from twenty feet away in the same way a person with normal vision can see that object from eighty feet away.[7]

Brown said the recipients of prayer often reported feeling heat, cold, or even tingling or itching as they were being healed.

But was it scientific? The only thing that changed between the pre-prayer and post-prayer tests was the fact that someone prayed to Jesus for the person to get better, and laid hands on them in prayer. Brown was ready with the answer.

"We had the proper equipment. We had a trained research team. We had statistically significant results," she says. "And the validity of the study was evaluated as being scientifically sound by the journal that published it. With a smaller sample [only twenty-four people were tested], the effects have to be larger and more consistent in order to achieve statistical significance. And our effects were."

Brown and her team then did a similar study in Brazil to check if they would get the same results. They did. Again, sight and hearing were improved after hands-on prayer was offered in Jesus' name.

One thirty-eight-year-old woman in southeastern Brazil could not count a person's fingers when they were held up from nine feet away. When she opened her eyes after prayer, she could not only count the fingers, she could read the nametag of the person who had been praying for her.

As I looked more at her studies, I had to admit that *something* was going on with prayer. This wasn't wishful thinking. It was not fakery. And it wasn't some "spiritual healer" on TV trying to get people to send in their money. These were documented cases of God's healing through prayer that were backed up by science.

The movement of God's power around the world warranted further investigation. Brown's research and results were amazing: God was supernaturally healing people. But as I dug deeper, I heard reports of Jesus appearing to people in dreams and visions—drawing them into a personal relationship with him.

It sounded like something straight out of the Bible, like when Jesus appeared to Saul and called him to stop persecuting and start serving God's kingdom. Sure, I believed the Bible story. But did God still appear to people today? I had to find out.

Questions About Miracles

1. Many scientists say prayers aren't effective for healing. Do you agree or disagree? Why? Should scholars try to study apparent miracles?

_____

_____

_____

2. What is your reaction to the prayer studies Candy Gunther Brown conducted in Mozambique and Brazil? Were you surprised by the sudden improvements right after prayer? Why?

_____

_____

3. If you could design a new study to try to determine whether miraculous healings have taken place, what might it look like?

_____

_____

_____

_____

4. Brown talks about the differences between prayers that are made from a distance verses prayers from up close. Why is this important?

_____

_____

5. Read the story of Peter and John healing a man who couldn't walk in Acts 3:1-8. What details do you notice in this story? Write down what stands out to you.

_____

_____

CHAPTER 6

DREAMS AND VISIONS

Kamal was busy at work when he felt God leading him to go to the Khan el-Khalili Market in Cairo. Kamal secretly started churches in Egypt. It was dangerous work in the Muslim country, where being a Christian could get you killed. The Friday market was the last place he wanted to go. This was right before Muslim prayers, and at that time of day the market was crowded, noisy, and chaotic. But he went because he felt one hundred

percent convinced that God had a special assign-
ment for him.

When he arrived at the market, a Muslim
woman named Noor[1], covered head to toe in tradi-
tional clothing, spotted him from a distance and
started yelling.

"You're the one! You're the one!" she shouted.

She pushed through the crowd and made a bee-
line for him.

"You were in my dream last night!" she said.
"Those clothes. You were wearing those clothes.
For sure, it was you."

Kamal quickly sensed what was happening. "Was
I with Jesus?" he asked.

"Yes," she replied. "Jesus was with us. Jesus
walked with me alongside a lake, and he told me how
much he loves me. His love was different from anything I've ever experienced. I've never felt so much
peace. I didn't want him to leave. I asked Jesus, 'Why
are you visiting me, a poor Muslim mother with eight
children?' And all he said was, 'I love you, Noor. I
have given everything for you. I died for you.'"

As Jesus turned to leave in her dream, he told
Noor, "Ask my friend tomorrow about me. He will
tell you all you need in order to understand why
I've visited you." Then Jesus pointed to Kamal,
who had been walking behind them in the dream.

There in the marketplace, Noor said to Kamal, "Even though you had walked with us around the lake, I hadn't seen anyone but Jesus. I thought I was alone with him. His face was magnificent. I couldn't take my eyes off him. Jesus did not tell me your name, but you were wearing the same clothes you have on right now, and your glasses—they're the same too. I knew I would not forget your smile."

Kamal and Noor found a safe place to talk. Their conversation about faith lasted three hours. Noor told Kamal that for the first time in her life, she didn't feel any fear or shame. "I felt ... perfect peace," she said.

Kamal explained to her that her religion will never bring her the peace she felt in her dream. That peace can only come from a relationship with Jesus.

"That's what [Jesus] wants to give you," Kamal

WORDS TO KNOW

Muslim: a person who follows the religion of Islam and believes in God, who they call Allah. Islam started in AD 610 and is the second most popular religion in the world. Only Christianity has more followers.

told her. "Before he went to the cross, Jesus said, 'Peace I leave with you; my peace I give you.'[2] You will not—cannot—find peace like that with anyone else. No one but Jesus even has it to offer."[3]

Was this a chance encounter? Was Noor's dream just the result of eating a spoiled piece of lamb kebab? Or was Jesus making himself known to someone who'd almost certainly never know him without a supernatural sign?

Noor is just one of countless Muslims who have experienced supernatural visions or dreams. After they experience these visions, many have converted from Islam and put their faith in Christ.

In fact, more Muslims have become Christians in the 21st century than in the previous fourteen hundred years combined. It's estimated that a quarter to a third of Muslims who convert to Christianity experienced a dream or vision of Jesus before praying to accept him as their Savior.[4] If those statistics are accurate, then this phenomenon of Jesus supernaturally appearing to people is one of the most significant spiritual awakenings in the world today.

In the Bible, God frequently used dreams and visions to further his plans. There are about two hundred biblical examples. From Abraham, Joseph, and Samuel in the Old Testament to Zacharias, John, and Cornelius in the New Testament, God often made himself known through divine intervention.

Today, reports of these miraculous appearances come from Muslims who live from Indonesia to Pakistan to the Gaza Strip. While the experiences are generally unique to the individual, sometimes two people have an identical dream on the same night.

In addition, the stunning consistency of these experiences across different countries—such as Jesus telling the person something in the dream that he or she could not otherwise have known—suggests that they are more than made-up stories. Plus, a devout Muslim would have no reason to imagine an encounter with the Jesus of Christianity. In some countries, when a Muslim becomes a Christian, he could be killed. So Muslims would have good reason *not* to dream about Jesus Christ.

But it is happening. A lot. And that leaves us with a lot of questions:

- Why is Jesus appearing to so many people in visions today?
- Why does he appear to people whose

religion so adamantly denies the truth of Christianity?

- What does Jesus tell these individuals that so radically rocks their world and causes them to risk their lives and follow him?

To get to the bottom of these questions, I turned to Tom Doyle. As a pastor for twenty years, Doyle served at churches in Dallas, Albuquerque, and Colorado Springs. Then, in 1995, Dallas Seminary called and said they were taking some pastors to Israel.

"That changed everything for me," Doyle says. "I was immediately drawn to the Middle East—hook, line, and sinker."

Over the next twenty years, he became a missionary to the region, eventually leading sixty tours of the Holy Land. Today, he is the founding president of UnCharted, a ministry dedicated to bringing Christians into the movement of God among Jews and Muslims. He's also written seven books about his expertise on the Middle East.

FROM TERRORIST TO CHURCH PLANTER

Doyle became aware of the phenomenon of dreams and visions among Islamic people during his first visit to Jerusalem. On that trip, he met with a group of Muslims who had converted to Christianity.

"One of them, Rami, said he had been a fervent Muslim when he started to have dreams about Jesus," Doyle says. "[Jesus] was a man in a white robe, and he told Rami that he loves him. They were beside a lake, and Rami said he saw himself walking over and embracing Jesus."

Rami said his normal dreams were often fuzzy and confused. But his dreams about Jesus were different than anything he had ever experienced. They were bright and laser-focused. And they kept coming.

At first Doyle thought Rami may have been crazy. But over and over, Doyle heard the same dream from different people: Jesus in a white robe, saying he loves them, saying he died for them, telling them to follow him. It started to snowball. He learned about people having dreams in Iran, Iraq, Syria . . . all over.

"I could pick up the phone right now, call Syria, and ask if our people have any stories about dreams," Doyle says, "and they would give me three or four new ones. That's how prevalent they are."

Recently, Doyle met a man named Omar in Jerusalem, who grew up in a Palestinian refugee camp. He hated Israel. He told Doyle that his goal in life was to kill as many Jews as he could. Years ago, as Omar was going to meet with members of the terrorist group Hamas, a man in a white robe suddenly stood before him in the street.

"Omar didn't know anything about Jesus," Doyle says. "But the man in the white robe pointed at him and said, 'Omar, this is not the life I have planned for you. You turn around. Go home. I have another plan for you.'"

Omar was stunned. He turned around and went home. Later that same day, someone moved into an apartment across the hall from him. The new person was a Christian. Omar told his new neighbor about the experience. This Christian spent time with Omar, took him through the Scriptures, and led him to Jesus. Today, Omar is an underground church planter.

"THAT'S HOW JESUS OPERATES"

Doyle shared numerous stories of radical life change. Many of the people lived in countries that were closed to Christianity. Missionaries weren't allowed in. These people had no prior exposure to images or ideas about the Jesus of the Bible.

The Qur'an, the holy book of Islam, *does* mention Jesus. It calls him a prophet, like Elijah. But the Qur'an denies that Jesus died on the cross or that he is the Son of God. So when Jesus tells followers of Islam that he died for them in these high-definition dreams, that's alien to everything Muslims have learned.

"I've never met someone who had a Jesus dream who is still hung up on the deity of Christ or the veracity of Scriptures," Doyle says. "Instantly, they know this: Jesus is more than just a prophet. They see Jesus for who he is and want to know more about him."

Doyle has also never heard of someone going to sleep as a Muslim, having a Jesus dream, and then waking up as a Christian. The dreams usually point them toward someone who can teach them from the Bible and present the gospel to them. That's what happened to Noor in the Cairo marketplace and Omar, who found a Christian moving in across the hall.

In the dreams, Jesus talks to them, and they feel love, grace, safety, protection, affirmation, joy, and peace—all emotions they don't receive from Islam.

"It rocks their world," Doyle says. "Just like Jesus did in the New Testament, he reached out to the marginalized: the Samaritan woman at the well, the blind and crippled, those with leprosy, the hated tax collector Zacchaeus. Today, who's more marginalized than Muslims? Jesus is showing his love for them. That's how Jesus operates."

SPREADING THE TRUTH

Jesus definitely operated that way when he appeared to Saul on the road to Damascus. That vision changed Saul's life. It even changed his name—to Paul. Then Paul's missionary journeys helped spread Christianity around the world. Doyle sees these dreams and visions working in a similar way.

It's estimated that 50 percent of Muslims around the world can't read. If they can't read, they'll never find the truth about Jesus in the Bible. And nearly nine out of ten Muslims don't know a Christian. So who's going to share the gospel with them?

Just like Jesus reached Saul through a vision to spread his message, God is doing the same thing in the Muslim world.

"It's hard to deny the evidence that something supernatural is happening," Doyle says. "Granted, it's the Word of God that leads people to faith, but these dreams plow the hard soil of Muslim hearts so they're receptive to the seed of the gospel."

Doyle does warn that every dream and vision shouldn't be accepted as fact. Everything needs to be checked against Scripture. *Does the dream line up with what we know about Jesus in the Bible?*

Another way to assess the legitimacy of these dreams is to measure the kind of fruit they bear.

WORDS TO KNOW

Unprecedented: never seen before in history; unparalleled

In other words, do they lead to a superficial and short-lived faith, or do they result in deep commitments to Christ?

"No question, these dreams generally lead to radical life-change," Doyle says. "A Muslim who comes to faith in the Middle East is exposing himself to possible rejection by his or her family, beatings, imprisonment, or even death."

Before praying with someone to receive Christ, many leaders in the Middle East will ask two questions:

1. First, are you willing to suffer for Jesus?
2. Second, are you willing to die for Jesus?

A dream or vision may start a person's journey toward Jesus. But their decision to follow Christ is carefully considered, especially with all the harsh potential consequences. Still, Muslims are coming to faith in Jesus in unprecedented numbers.

After talking with Doyle, I was impressed with the evidence and the impact dreams and visions are having around the world, especially in the Middle East. At the same time, I was also thankful that God had given me—and the world, really—the Bible, that tells me about Jesus. I have also his Spirit to affirm and guide me.

Jesus may not appear to a lot of people in North America in dreams and visions, but certainly a lot of Christians can say they felt the nudging of the Spirit to talk with somebody about Jesus in a restaurant or show kindness to somebody who's hurting.

Yet as I thought about my own life, I realized we don't talk about these promptings much. God's at work, but it's almost like we're embarrassed by it.

Being embarrassed or confused by something we don't understand is natural. And when it comes to the *supernatural,* there's a lot we don't understand.

To dig deeper, I knew my next step was to find out why many Christians are embarrassed to talk about the supernatural events that happen in their lives.

Questions About Miracles

1. Do you believe God sometimes guides people through dreams? Have you ever had a dream that you believe came from beyond yourself? Describe your experience.

_____

_____

_____

2. What are some dangers of Christians focusing too much on dreams or feelings? How can you make sure you're not being misled?

_____

_____

3. In the Middle East, a person who comes to faith in Christ is often asked two things:
   - Are willing to suffer for Jesus?
   - Are you willing to die for him?

   Honestly, how would you answer those questions?

_____

_____

_____

4. Why do you think God is using dreams and visions to reach people with his love in the Middle East, but we don't often see similar events in America?

_____

CHAPTER 7

EMBARRASSED BY THE SUPERNATURAL

A ten-year-old boy and his family were driving down the road. He was fidgety and tired from the long drive. As he played around in the backseat of the car, the door accidentally flew open, and the boy fell out. (Note: This happened before laws that said children have to wear seat belts in cars.)

Shocked and scared, the boy's father slammed on the brakes. His parents jumped out of the car and ran back to where their son had fallen. They were sure he'd be dead or at the very least in need of emergency medical treatment.

But instead of finding their son injured and lying in the road, he was standing next to the road like nothing had happened.

"What happened?" the boy's parents said. "Are you okay?

"I'm fine," the boy answered. "Didn't you see the man? He caught me."

The parents *hadn't* seen anybody. They'd feared the worst, because kids just don't fall out of cars without being injured. Even if there was a man by the side of the road, how could he amazingly catch their son ... and where was the man now?

Yet *somebody* must have saved their son. He was talking and standing there without a scratch. The parents' conclusion: God supernaturally intervened.

Was this boy just lucky? Did he have the makings of a natural-born Hollywood stuntman? Or is it possible an angel caught him?[1]

Even as a Christian, there have been times when I've been hesitant to talk openly about supernatural events that have happened in my life. It's not that I don't believe God still does miracles. I just don't want to be seen as weird.

Whether it's because of Hollywood films or radical news stories, many people in modern-day society think Christians act strangely. All many people know about Christianity is a movie version where followers of God are portrayed as an oddball preacher, a phony faith-healer, an overly emotional evangelist, or a money-grubbing pastor.

That's not a true picture. Christians come in all shapes and sizes. We work many different types of jobs. There are rock-solid followers of Christ in professional sports, Hollywood, the government, big business, colleges, coffee shops, music, and every other line of work.

For the most part, we're not weird. And we often try extra hard not to be viewed that way. We want our friends and classmates to see us as normal people. We usually don't talk about the miraculous, since it seems odd to the world.

So when I saw a blog post titled "Embarrassed by the Supernatural," I didn't even have to read it. I knew I had to talk to the author, Roger E. Olson.

Olson served as a youth minister, earned a Ph.D. in religious studies, and has written numerous books. Today, he's a professor of Christian Theology of Ethics at George W. Truett Theological Seminary at Baylor University.

I was drawn to the fact that Olson had

experience in different Christian circles. He'd attended churches where people believe miracles happen every day. And he was also familiar with groups that say God stopped doing miracles after Bible times. I figured he would be a good source of wisdom when it came to figuring out why Christians are embarrassed about supernatural occurrences of God's power, and I wasn't disappointed.

ACT LIKE ACTS

When Olson looks at the church in America, he sees a lot of people relying on their own human knowledge and reason. They don't allow God to guide their lives, because they've already made up their minds. They act like they don't need God to move in their lives anymore. Maybe you've seen this with your friends or acted this way yourself. You say you're a follower of Christ, but your words and actions are like everybody else's.

Instead of trying to live like the rest of society, Olson encourages Christians to follow God's wisdom and the promptings of the Holy Spirit. But that's not easy.

"There's a certain unpredictability with the Holy Spirit," Olson says. "Many Christians don't want any big surprises. We don't want to open the door to something that will really shock us, because we can't control it. To me, the book of Acts is the best guide."

The book of Acts tells the story of the early church. It follows Jesus' disciples starting from Jesus' ascension into heaven. The book is filled with stories of God's miracles. From Peter being rescued from jail by an angel to Paul surviving a shipwreck and deadly snakebite, the disciples saw God's hand on their everyday lives. Through his power, the disciples healed the blind, brought people back from the dead, and boldly proclaimed the truth about Jesus. They weren't shy about telling stories of Jesus' miracles and his resurrection. The apostles seemed to go around expecting that when they told somebody about Jesus, something supernatural might very well occur.

But that's not true today.

Whether we recognize it or not, many American Christians have put Jesus in a box. We believe miraculous events happened in the past (biblical times) and in other countries (mission fields), but we don't see them as an ever-present possibility in our lives.

"This is obvious from the way we react when someone gets sick," Olson says. "Of course, we pray for them, but what do we ask? That God would comfort them in the midst of their suffering. That

God would guide the hands of surgeons. That God would give doctors wisdom and discernment. But the Bible says to pray for their healing, lay hands on them, and anoint them with oil."

To illustrate his point, Olson told a story about an encounter he had with a pastor whose wife is a medical doctor. As they shared different ways they saw God working in their lives, the pastor lowered his voice and said quietly, "You know, my daughter was very sick and I anointed her with oil and prayed fervently for her, and she was healed. It was absolutely supernatural."

At the time Olson remembers thinking, *Why are we whispering?*

God's power should be shouted from the rooftops, not whispered about so nobody can hear.

DESPERATE TO FIT IN

Olson tried to come up with one word to summarize why a lot Christians seem embarrassed by the supernatural. He gave it some thought and then said, "Respectability."

In other words, we want to show that we're smart and refined. We don't want to be looked at as gullible or superstitious—like the over-the-top Christians our friends have seen on television. We want to show we've got everything under control.

Because of this, we internalize our view of God. We keep what we believe about him to ourselves. Yes, we want to have a relationship with Jesus . . . but just in our inner life, not with the outside world.

Living in this way makes us blend in with everybody else. Instead of earning respect, it causes disregard. Nobody cares what we believe, because they have no idea about our beliefs.

God doesn't call us to blend in. He calls us to stand up and stand out for him. If God is omnipotent—which means he's all-powerful—then it makes sense that he's going to continue to act in his world, and we need to tell people about it.

Olson's classes at Baylor University in Texas attract students from around the globe in addition to students from the Unites States. As he teaches these students from Third World countries, he often notices their attitude about Christianity and the supernatural is quite different than his students from the United States.

Christianity in Africa is filled with stories of God intervening and doing amazing things. Olson once invited a priest from Nigeria to address his class. For an hour and twenty minutes, this man talked about God's supernatural actions in Nigeria. The students were in awe.

"It lit a fire in their faith," Olson says. "We need the supernatural as much as they do in China. America is still a mission field."

GENTLE WHISPERS OF GOD

Olson is also quick to point out that not all miracles are spectacular healings of incurable diseases. Not every supernatural intervention is as earth-shattering as someone rising from the dead. More often, God's speaks in gentle whispers, or he orchestrates everyday events in a way that sends a message of encouragement, correction, or hope when we desperately need it.

Many Christians experience these subtle "leadings" or "impressions" from God. But, again, we often don't talk about them for fear of the skeptical reaction we'll get from our friends. So we keep quiet, embarrassed by the supernatural.

Olson strongly believes that God continues to "speak" to his people today. We hear from him in

WORDS TO KNOW

Skeptical: doubting that a statement or experience is true the Bible as well as through inaudible promptings from his Spirit, who lives in us. God may nudge us to sit with the new kid at lunch. He might prompt us to pray for a sick relative. Or maybe he calls us to do something nice for a bully. We may never know the outcomes of these gentle whispers, but they certainly make life more exciting.

One day, a nine-year-old boy in Tennessee was eating breakfast at a restaurant with his family. Another family sat at a table next to them. In his heart, the boy felt like he needed to share his story with the family at the other table.

"Mom, can I go tell them about my life?" he asked his mom. "Will you please come with me?"

His mom agreed. The two of them got up and walked to the next table.

"Hi, my name is Isaiah," the boy said, raising his shirt to show them the scars that covered his chest and abdomen. "I want to tell you about my life. I was born ten weeks early and spent almost the whole first year of my life in the hospital. I had thirteen surgeries. I also went into liver failure. My parents were told I would die, but Jesus saved my life!"

A young man sitting at the table looked stunned. He lifted his shirt and pointed to the scars on his chest. "I was also born early and had open heart surgery as a baby," he said. "I was supposed to die too."

His parents started to cry. The family thanked the nine-year-old for having the courage to come over and share his story.[2]

While Olson is aware that skeptics label these "God things" as coincidence or "lucky timing," he's seen how these perfectly timed promptings can change lives forever.

Of course, the results may not be life changing at all. We may pray for a sick relative who never gets better. Sometimes the bully keeps being mean, despite our best efforts. A miracle doesn't always happen. God doesn't appear to show up every time we ask for a healing. Many Christians are uncomfortable with the supernatural, because they don't want to be embarrassed if an answer doesn't come.

Again, Olson points to Acts as a guide for how we should act. God didn't always answer with a miracle in the Bible either. Sometimes his followers lost their lives because they spoke out for Christ. Later in the New Testament, the apostle Paul talks about having a thorn in the flesh that God never healed despite many prayers. In the midst of all that, the early church kept praying, kept following, and kept trusting God.

"God is sovereign and not arbitrary," Olson says. "He knows what he's doing. When he doesn't answer our prayers as we want, there may be particularities about the situation that we just don't understand."

Still, when God appears to *not* answer, it hurts. When a loved one we prayed for dies, we can doubt God's goodness. Any credible look at miracles must deal with the ones that never happen. And that was the last step I had to take on this journey.

Questions About Miracles

1.   Have you ever had what you thought was a supernatural experience, but you were afraid to share because you didn't want others to think you were a religious weirdo? Please tell the story. If nothing like this has ever happened to you, can you understand why some Christians are uncomfortable sharing their experience? Why or why not?

_____

_____

2.   Have you seen examples of people in your church or other Christians who say they believe in God but who live as if God's plan and guidance doesn't matter to them? Have you ever acted this way yourself? Explain.

_____

_____

3. Roger E. Olson said the quest for respectability prompts some Christians to feel embarrassed by the supernatural. "We are desperate to fit in," he said. What do you think of this statement? Do you agree or disagree? Why?

_____

_____

_____

4. The gentle nudging of the Holy Spirit can lead us into some exciting and unpredictable situations. Can you describe an experience where you believe God was leading you? How can you become more aware of these leadings by God's Spirit?

_____

_____

Dear Diary,
No miracle today.
MY DIARY 2018
Dear Diary,
Still waiting for a miracle.
MY DIARY 2078

CHAPTER 8

WHEN MIRACLES DON'T HAPPEN

Tricia Lott Williford's husband died unexpectedly after a twelve-hour illness. She had two young children who hadn't even started kindergarten. Now she was a widow and single mother. She had prayed for her husband during his tragic illness. She asked for a miracle to save his life, and God had answered with a no.

"When God gives to other people in a way he hasn't given to you, it's easy to feel left out," she

WORDS TO KNOW

Sovereignty: having supreme power, control, and authority

says, "and it's hard to want to hear how good he has been to other people. . . But faith is not measured by our ability to manipulate God to get what *we want*. It is measured by our willingness to submit to what *He wants*."

Williford says there's no formula we can use that guarantees Jesus will say yes. That's the thing with sovereignty: God gets to decide yes, no, if, when, and how. All we can do is pray, trust, and have confidence in his faithfulness.

"Miracles are temporary," Williford adds. "But the word of Jesus, his teachings—they bring eternal life. Real life. Your faith in him, your belief that he is real, even when the miracle isn't yours, even when he doesn't say yes to you—this is what brings eternal life."[1]

While researching this book, I came across inspiring examples of how God miraculously restored sight to the blind, hearing to the deaf, and life to the dead. I celebrated when God chose to supernaturally intervene and show his power in creation.

But throughout my life, I've also seen many times when God didn't answer prayer with a miracle. Not every student who prays for help on a test receives a dream from God that shows a figure writing all the answers on the board. Often when we pray for God's help on a test that we didn't study for, we fail.

Every lost pet that gets prayed for doesn't return home safely. Every sick person who's lifted before the Lord isn't miraculously healed. We live in a fallen world. Until we're in heaven with Jesus, we may never understand why certain things happen.

The Bible explains that God's ways are above our understanding. The Lord told the prophet Isaiah: "For my thoughts are not your thoughts, neither are your ways my ways. As the heavens are higher than the earth, so are my ways higher than your ways and my thoughts than your thoughts."[2]

In the pages of this book, we've seen that God still supernaturally restores life and health to the ailing. But if we try to control his power, harness it, predict it, or fully understand it, it invariably ends in frustration.

Even Jesus didn't heal every person he met. When Jesus was in Nazareth, Matthew's gospel says, "He did not do many miracles there because of their lack of faith."[3] The disciples were given authority to heal in Matthew 10, and yet seven chapters later they failed to heal an epileptic boy.[4] Paul didn't heal everyone either. The Bible says he left Trophimus sick in Miletus.[5] So there are biblical reasons behind why we shouldn't be surprised when everyone isn't healed.

In order to avoid being frustrated, we have to move away from trying to explain why a particular individual wasn't healed or why a certain miracle didn't happen. That's God's business. All we know is that God asked us to pray for the people in our lives, and we can request healing for those people. We just have to be obedient and trust.

At the same time, God is not asking us to turn off our brains or not ask tough questions. But in the end, he *does* ask us to trust him. That can be challenging, especially when we're hurting and feel like God's far away.

Douglas R. Groothuis (pronounced GROTE-hice) knows what it means to deal with hurt in his life. His father died in an airplane crash when he was eleven. Although he was taught as a youngster to believe in God, he followed other religions during his teens. Finally, at age nineteen, he decided to faithfully follow Christ and was baptized.

Groothuis went on to earn his doctorate in philosophy at the University of Oregon. He served as a campus pastor for a dozen years before joining the faculty of Denver Seminary in 1993. Since then, he has published thirteen books.

More recently, he's dealt with the challenges of caring for his ailing wife, who was diagnosed with a progressive, incurable, and eventually fatal brain disease. Groothuis has prayed for a miracle in his wife's life, but so far he's only seen her steadily decline.

Through all these heartbreaking circumstances, he has continued to cling to God and his promises. I knew he'd be the perfect person to talk to about how to handle it when God doesn't do a miracle.

LOST ART OF THE LAMENT

Groothuis began by stating that it's rational to believe in miracles. When he looks at the Earth and all its beauty and fine-tuning, he believes there's a creator. He has studied the historical evidence for miracles, including the resurrection of Jesus, and found it to be reliable.

WORDS TO KNOW

Rational: based on reason and using the mind's intellect

The miracle of Jesus rising from the dead can bring hope to those who are going through suffering. First, because we know that God can relate to our pain. He understands what it's like to have a loved one die. But even more amazingly, God can take the very worst thing that could ever happen in the universe—the death of his Son on a cross— and turn it into the very best thing ever to happen in the universe—the opening of heaven for all who follow him. If he can do that, then he is more than able to take our difficult circumstances and draw good from them, if we trust in him.[6]

Then there's Joseph's story in Genesis. His brothers betrayed him and sold him into slavery. He was falsely accused and imprisoned in Egypt. Yet God put him in one of the most powerful positions in the known world. So when his brothers went to Egypt to beg for food, Joseph could truthfully say, "You intended to harm me, but God intended it for good" (Genesis 50:20).

As we go through difficult times, we may not know what good God is achieving in the short run. But given the credibility of Christianity and the truth of the Bible, we can believe there is significance and purpose in suffering.

"We can't read the mind of God," Groothuis says. "We're not privy to why he chooses to work a miracle in some cases and not others. Yes, it can be agonizing when you've prayed and fasted for the healing of a loved one and God seems to have said no or to wait until eternity."

By dealing with all the loss in his life, Groothuis says he's learned to lament. There are many biblical examples of lamenting. Sixty of the Psalms are laments. There's lament in Ecclesiastes and Job. Jesus laments over the unbelief of Jerusalem. On the cross, his lament came as the cry, "My God, my God, why have you forsaken me?"[7]

"Look," Groothuis says, "God's good world has

WORDS TO KNOW

Lament: expressing great sorrow, grief, or weeping over tragic events or circumstances been broken by sin, and it's morally and spiritually right to lament the loss of a true good. I'm grateful for the lament we see in Scripture—it's God helping us learn how to suffer well."

Although "suffering well" may sound like a strange thing to say, it's an important characteristic to develop, especially when God doesn't send a miracle. To suffer well, Groothuis says to:

1. Admit your grief
2. Pray, even when you're not feeling like you want to
3. Be honest with God
4. Not stuff down your emotions

Lamenting can be tear-filled and messy. But it can also help us work through losses in our lives, while clinging to God.

Throughout the Psalms, David cries out to God and shows his emotions. He was angry at God and felt like God had left him. But after expressing his emotion, David always turned back to the goodness of God.

Groothuis has gone through similar feelings while dealing with his pain. "I never questioned whether God exists, but I confess that there were times when I questioned his goodness," he says. "In the end, I know too much to think that God isn't perfectly good. I'm grateful he allows us to vent our frustration. Read Ecclesiastes or the psalms of lament. They are startlingly honest."

God is big enough, strong enough, and caring enough to handle our honesty. He wants us to share our hurts, frustrations, and feelings with him.

Sadly, some people turn away from God when they pray for a miracle and it doesn't happen.

Groothuis understands those feelings, but encourages people to think about Jesus during their darkest times.

"When I'm distressed and anguished at my circumstances, I think of Christ hanging on the cross for me," he says. "This brings me back to spiritual sanity. Jesus suffered far more than you or I ever will. He endured the torture of the crucifixion out of his love for me. He didn't have to do that. He chose to. So he doesn't just sympathize with us in

WORDS TO KNOW

Empathize: the ability to better understand what somebody is feeling by putting yourself in their shoes our suffering; he empathizes with us. Ultimately, I find comfort in that."

FAITHFULNESS THROUGH SUFFERING

All suffering isn't the same. Groothuis says it's important to remember the difference between *meaningless* suffering and *inscrutable* suffering.

- Meaningless suffering means suffering that is simply there. It doesn't achieve a greater good; it has no purpose.
- Inscrutable suffering means we don't know what the purpose is, but we have reason to believe that God is providential, loving, and all-powerful. Our suffering may seem meaningless to us, but it's not.

God uses the bad in our lives for a greater good that could not be achieved otherwise. The Bible even tells us to "glory in our sufferings." God in his infinite, unlimited power and wisdom uses suffering to produce perseverance. Perseverance helps our character to grow. Having a strong character results in hope.[8]

And it's hope in God's faithfulness and good plan for our lives that gets us through the times that we pray and then don't see a miracle.

Groothuis says you may feel lonely or empty when God doesn't supernaturally intervene. But one way or another, God gets the glory—and that's always a good thing (even when it doesn't feel that way).

"God gets the glory when somebody is miraculously healed," Groothuis explains, "and he also gets the glory when someone develops faithfulness and character through suffering."

Another thing we should keep in mind is that Jesus' faithfulness was shown through his suffering. On the night he was arrested, Jesus went to the garden of Gethsemane with his disciples. Jesus was overwhelmed with sorrow and grief. He knew God had sent him to die for all of humanity's sins. But the task was overwhelming—even to the Son of God. Jesus asked the Father to rescue him from the fate of the cross. He was basically asking for a miracle. Then Jesus prayed another prayer. He said, "May your will be done."[9]

Jesus put himself totally in his Father's hands. Whatever his Father had in store for him was what he wanted for himself. And that's the same attitude we need to have. As difficult as it might be at the time, we have to say, "Lord, whatever you have in store for me is what I want." In a sense, it's a prayer of obedience, of submission, of trust, and of faith.

We can also have faith in God's promise in Romans 8:28. God can—and will—cause good to emerge from the difficulties of life, if we are faithful to him.

So even when it feels like we're hanging by a thread, we can have confidence knowing that the thread is spun by the God of miracles.

There's no easy answer to why God sometimes displays his power and other times he doesn't. By definition, miracles are outside the normal course of events. They're a supernatural exception to the way the world usually works. Though they're more common than we may think, they're still relatively rare—which means for most people, a sudden and complete healing isn't going to happen. But that doesn't mean God is absent. During my talk with Groothuis, he made that fact abundantly clear.

He also made it crystal clear that an abundant life can only come through a relationship with Jesus.[10] God doesn't cast us adrift to face our struggles on our own. He walks with us on our journey through life, even when we walk through the darkest valley.[11]

And I had walked a long way in my investigation into miracles. Now it was time for me to take the final step on my journey: I had to make up my mind about what I truly believed.

Questions About Miracles

1. Have you ever prayed to God for a miracle in your life or for a family member or friend, but the miracle you requested never came? Describe what happened. How did you react? What emotions did you feel? How did this affect your view of God?

_____

_____

_____

_____

2. Douglas Groothuis said when life gets really hard for him, it helps to think about Jesus hanging on the cross so all people who turn to God could know him personally and be forgiven. Why do you think Jesus' sacrifice makes life better?

_____

_____

_____

_____

_____

3. What kind of "significance and purpose" do you believe can be found in our suffering? What good might God draw from such experiences?

_____

_____

_____

_____

4. Groothuis draws a distinction between mean-ingless suffering and inscrutable suffering. How would you describe the difference between them? Was this definition helpful for you? In what way?

_____

_____

_____

_____

CONCLUSION

REACHING YOUR VERDICT

Of the thousands of dreams I had as a kid, I only remember one of them now. I'm still amazed by its clarity and vibrancy, as well as the emotional impact it had on me at the time. It was the most dramatic—and puzzling—dream of my growing-up years. While it wasn't an encounter with Jesus, it was a dream in which I spoke with an angel. The angel told me something that confused me at the time, but came true sixteen years later.

When I was about twelve years old, I dreamed I was making a sandwich in the kitchen. (Okay, I admit the dream had a boring beginning.) Suddenly, an angel appeared and started telling me how wonderful and glorious heaven is. I listened for a while. Then I said matter-of-factly, "I'm going there."

The angel's reply stunned me. "How do you know?"

How did I know? What kind of question is that? I thought in the dream.

But I managed to stammer to the angel, "Well, uh, I've tried to be a good kid. I've tried to do what my parents say. I've tried to behave. I've been to church."

"That doesn't matter," the angel said.

Now I was staggered. *How could all my efforts to be good, do the right thing, and live up to the expectations of my parents not matter?* Panic rose in me.

The angel studied me for a few moments. Then he said, "Someday you'll understand." Instantly, he was gone, and I woke up in a sweat.

At the time, I believed people earned their way into heaven through good deeds. I thought if I did more good things than bad—or even more good things than most people—certainly God would let me into his kingdom. But as time passed, I came to reject the possibility of the supernatural and even God himself. I lived as an atheist for a long period of time, even forgetting the dream, during my college days and early in my career as a journalist.

Then sixteen years after the dream, the angel's words came true. In a suburban Chicago church, I heard the message of grace and *understood* what it meant for the first time. I couldn't earn my way to heaven. Eternal life was a free gift from God. It was about God's grace, not my performance. All I needed to do was receive his gift in repentance and faith.

The moment this clicked for me, a vivid memory popped into my mind—it was the angel! God had let me know as a twelve-year-old that someday I would understand the gospel. Ultimately, it was this good news that changed my life and my eternity.

Was my dream a supernatural intervention? Would it qualify as a miracle? I'll leave it to you to make your own judgment.

PERSUADED BY THE EVIDENCE

I'll also leave it up to you to decide what you believe about miracles. My journey in building a case for miracles filled my office—and then my living room—with file folders, textbooks, yellow legal pads with countless notes, and stacks of interview transcripts.

I had started with a definition for miracles offered by writer and professor Richard L. Purtill. For an event to be a true miracle, he said it had to be brought about by the power of God to create a temporary exception to the ordinary course of nature, for the purpose of showing that God acts in history.

After talking with physicist Michael Strauss, I found myself even more convinced that the origin and fine-tuning of the universe pointed powerfully toward the existence of a supernatural Creator—and an amazing miracle of creation.

I looked over Craig Keener's gigantic study of miracles. I was impressed by all the astounding instances of supernatural intervention in which there were multiple, reliable eyewitnesses, medical documentation, and a lack of motivation to lie. Could some of the examples be explained away by naturalistic arguments? *Probably.* But could all of them? *Not by a long shot.*

Then there were the facts of history, cited by detective J. Warner Wallace. He established that Jesus of Nazareth not only claimed to be the unique Son of God, but then he proved it by returning from the dead. Talk about a miracle!

In fact, the resurrection goes beyond confirming the existence of the miracles. The willingness of Jesus to endure the crucifixion tells us that God will take extraordinary action to rescue his creation from the consequences of their sins. And if he loves us *that* much, then it's reasonable to believe he would choose to use his power in other ways throughout history, such as miraculously healing someone who is suffering.

Candy Gunther Brown's research showed instant improvements in eyesight and hearing after hands-on prayer by sincere followers of Jesus. Other scientific studies point toward prayer as having a positive impact on healing.

And I couldn't ignore all the extraordinary dreams and visions that were reported by missionary Tom Doyle. Many of the dreams caused people who were opposed to Christianity to accept the truth of God's love when they encountered specific individuals they had only seen in an earlier vision. These stories weren't just mere coincidence. God was up to something.

Something supernatural, you might say.

THE MOST VALUABLE MIRACLE OF ALL

Believing in miracles doesn't mean you have to accept every supernatural claim that gets splashed across the magazine covers you see in the grocery store. But every "miraculous" event should be examined. This is standard practice for lawyers, judges, journalists, detectives, historians, juries, and others who are authentically trying to pursue the truth.

Before you buy into a miracle claim, consider the witness's character, his motives, his biases; seek medical documentation or other corroborating evidence wherever possible; and make sure the event lines up with God's character and actions in the Bible.

Christianity *invites* investigation . . . so do miracles. When the Gospels report supernatural events, they aren't introduced with, "Once upon a time. . . ." Rather, they're reported with specific details and within a historical context that can be checked out and verified.

After nearly two years of research, I came to my own verdict about miracles: they're often credible and convincing, and they contribute powerfully to the case for Christ. As a judge in a court of appeals would say: *the verdict is affirmed.*

And if Christ is real and Christianity is true, then there's an even more important verdict we all must reach. It's a decision that answers the question raised by the angel who appeared in my dream all those years ago: "How do you know that you'll go to heaven?"

The merit-based system of salvation that I grew up believing doesn't work. There's no way we can live up to God's standard. Even if we give our lives completely to serve the poor, sacrifice everything, and live a wholly selfless existence, it doesn't measure up to God's standard of perfection. That's something none of us can attain through our efforts.

Thankfully, God gives us *grace*—a free gift of forgiveness and eternal life to all who receive it in repentance and faith.[1] That's what Jesus' death and resurrection were all about: paying the penalty we deserve for our lies and wrongdoings.[2]

That's the most valuable miracle of all.

Each of us must make our own decision to receive or decline God's gift. As you think about the contents of this book, I trust that you will keep an open mind and a receptive heart. It's my hope that you will be encouraged by this promise of Proverbs:

"If you scream for insight and call loudly for understanding, if you pursue it like you would money, and search it out as you would hidden treasure, then the Lord will be awesome to you, and you will come into possession of the knowledge of God."[3]

Questions About Miracles

1. Which chapter in this book makes the strongest case for miracles? Why? Go back and look, then write down your answer.

_____

_____

_____

2. After reading this book, are you convinced that God continues to supernaturally intervene in people's lives? Why?

_____

_____

3. Many people think they can earn their way to heaven through good actions. (That's what I thought as a twelve-year-old boy.) But Romans 3:23 warns that "all have sinned and fall short of the glory of God." The Bible makes it clear that salvation cannot be earned by our good deeds, but must be received as a gift of grace through faith. Romans 6:23 explains, "For the wages of sin is death, but the gift of God is eternal life in Christ Jesus our Lord." Have you taken that step? If not, why not do so now and pray this prayer:

"Jesus, I believe eternal life is something that only comes from you. I can't earn my way into heaven through good behavior. Thank you for dying for my sins and miraculously raising from the dead. You are the God of miracles, and one of the biggest miracles is that I can be forgiven and live with you forever in heaven. I accept your gift of salvation and commit my life to you. Help me to follow you. Amen."

If you just prayed that prayer, don't keep it a secret. You've just reached the most important verdict of your life. Tell a parent, pastor, friend, or the person who gave you this book. They'll want to celebrate with you the miracle of new life that you've found in Jesus Christ.

ABOUT THE AUTHORS

MEET LEE STROBEL

Lee Strobel, the former award-winning legal editor of *The Chicago Tribune*, is a *New York Times* bestselling author of more than twenty books. He formerly taught First Amendment Law at Roosevelt University and currently serves as Professor of Christian Thought at Houston Baptist University.

Lee was educated at the University of Missouri (Bachelor of Journalism degree) and Yale Law School (Master of Studies in Law degree). He was a journalist for fourteen years at *The Chicago Tribune* and other newspapers, winning Illinois's highest honor for public service journalism from United Press International.

After examining the evidence for Jesus, Lee became a Christian in 1981. He subsequently became a teaching pastor at two of America's most influential churches. Now he is a teaching pastor at Woodlands Church in Texas.

Lee has won national awards for his books *The Case for Christ, The Case for Faith, The Case for a*

Creator, and *The Case for Grace*. In 2017, his spiritual journey was depicted in a major motion picture, *The Case for Christ*.

Lee and Leslie have been married for forty-five years. Their daughter, Alison, is a novelist. Their son, Kyle, is a professor of spiritual theology at the Talbot School of Theology at Biola University.

MEET JESSE FLOREA

Jesse Florea has written and edited for Focus on the Family for nearly twenty-five years, where he oversees *Clubhouse* and *Clubhouse Jr.* magazines. He also cohosts the top-rated "Official Adventures in Odyssey" podcast. He has written, co-written, or edited more than thirty books, including *The Case for Grace for Kids* and *The Case for Grace for Kids: 90-Day Devotional*. Jesse earned bachelor and master's degrees in communications from Wheaton College. He lives with his wife, Stephanie, in Colorado Springs and enjoys hanging out with his two grown children, their spouses, and his granddaughter.

SOURCE INFORMATION FOR THE CASE FOR MIRACLES FOR KIDS

Epigraph

1. C. S. Lewis, *God in the Dock* (Grand Rapids, Mich.: Eerdmans, 2014), 13.
2. Eric Metaxas, *Miracles* (New York: Dutton, 2014), 16.
3. G. K. Chesterton, *The Innocence of Father Brown* (London, UK: Cassell and Co., 1911), 2.

Introduction

1. For a good analysis of this issue, see: John Piper, "Are Signs and Wonders for Today?" *Desiring God*, February 25, 1990. www.desiringgod.org/messages/are-signs-and-wonders-for-today.
2. A random, representative study of 1,000 U.S. adults completed this questionnaire. The sample error is +/- 3.1 percent points at the 95 percent confidence level. The response rate was 55 percent. The survey was conducted as the research for this book began in 2015.
3. Based on 2016 U.S. government estimate of population over the age of 18 at 249,454,440. See: www.census.gov/quickfacts/fact/table/US/.
4. This survey was conducted by HCD Research and the Louis Finkelstein Institute for Religious and Social Studies of the Jewish Theological Seminary. See: "Science of Miracle," *BusinessWire*, Dec. 20, 2004. www.businesswire.com/news/home/20041220005244/en/Science-Miracle-Holiday-Season-Survey-Reveals-Physicians.
5. Ibid.

Chapter 1

1. Anugrah Kumar, "Ben Carson Says God Helped Him Ace College Chemistry Exam by Giving Answers in a Dream," *Christian Post*, May 9, 2015. www.christianpost .com/news/ben-carson-says-God-helped-him-ace -college-chemistry-exam-by-giving-answers-in-dream -138913.
2. Richard L. Purtill, "Defining Miracles," in: Douglas Geivett and Gary R. Habermas, editors, *In Defense of Miracles* (Downers Grove, IL: InterVarsity, 1997), 72.

Chapter 2

1. "For since the creation of the world God's invisible qualities—his eternal power and divine nature—have been clearly seen, being understood from what has been made, so that men are without excuse." Romans 1:20.
2. Cambridge astrophysicist Geraint F. Lewis and Luke A. Barnes, a Cambridge-educated postdoctoral researcher at the Sydney Institute for Astronomy, responded to the claim, "Fine-tuning has been debunked," by replying: "No. It hasn't." Barnes reviewed the scientific literature on the topic, summarizing the conclusions of more than two hundred published papers in the field. "On balance, the fine-tuning of the Universe for life has stood up well under the scrutiny of physicists," they wrote. They added that it is "not the case" that "fine-tuning is the invention of a bunch of religious believers who hijacked physics to their own ends." Rather, they said, "Physics has tended to consolidate our understanding of fine-tuning." See: Geraint F. Lewis and Luke A. Barnes, *A Fortune Universe*, 241-243.

3. Peter D. Ward and Donald Brownlee, *Rare Earth* (New York: Copernicus, 2000), 220. For an excellent discussion of the importance of plate tectonics, see 191-220.

4. Hugh Ross, "Probability for Life on Earth," *Reasons to Believe*, April 1, 2004. www.reasons.org/articles/probability-for-life-on-earth. Also see: Hugh Ross, *Improbable Planet* (Grand Rapids, MI: Baker, 2016).

5. Besides, Strauss added, even if it turns out the multiverse idea is true, it would actually support the case for a Creator. Why? He explained: "Not only would the Borde-Guth-Vilenkin theorem point toward a beginning that would need a creator, but the extra dimensions of string theory would require that any creator exist in multiple dimensions. That would mean he could easily perform miraculous acts in our four dimensions. In fact, a discovery of other universes or extra dimensions would, in some sense, increase the necessary magnitude of any creator. One could legitimately ask the question, 'How many universes would an infinite God create?'"

Chapter 3

1. Helen Roseveare, *Living Faith* (Minneapolis, MN: Bethany House, 1980), 44-45, excerpted in: J.P. Moreland, *Kingdom Triangle* (Grand Rapids, MI: Zondervan, 2007), 17-19.

2. Gardner was a Fellow of the Royal College of Obstetricians and Gynecologists and of the Association of Surgeons in East Africa. He served as an examiner to the University of Newcastle-upon-Tyne. He was ordained by the United Free Church of Scotland. See: Rex Gardner, *Healing Miracles: A Doctor Investigates* (London: Darton, Longman and Todd, 1986), back cover.

3. Ibid., 202-205.

4. Edmond Tang, "'Yellers' and Healers–Pentecostalism and the Study of Grassroots Christianity in China," in: Allan Anderson and Edmond Tang, editors, *Asian and Pentecostal: The Charismatic Face of Christianity in Asia* (Oxford: Wipf & Stock, Revised Edition, 2011), 481.

5. Jim Rutz, *MegaShift* (Colorado Springs, CO: Empowerment, 2005), 4.

Chapter 4

1. Interview with Brock Eastman for magazine article in *Focus on the Family Clubhouse,* published October 2017, pp. 20-21.

2. John 21:25: "Jesus also did many other things. If they were all written down, I suppose the whole world could not control the books that would be written."

3. See: "Forensic Statement Analysis: Deception Detection," *Law Enforcement Learning*, undated. www.lawenforcementlearning.com/course/ forensic-statement-analysis.

4. See: Luke 1:1-3.

5. Interview for this book with Dr. Craig S. Keener.

6. See: 1 Corinthians 15:3ff.

7. See: Matthew 26:67-68.

8. See: Gary R. Habermas and Michael R. Licona, *The Case for the Resurrection of Jesus* (Grand Rapids, MI: Kregel, 2004).

9. See: John 19:34.

10. See: John 20:16-17, 20:27.

11. See: John 21:12.

12. Acts, Clement of Rome, Polycarp, Ignatius, Dionysius of Corinth (quoted by Eusebius), Tertullian, and Origen.

Chapter 5

1. Interview with Angela Bailey on November 1, 2017.
2. See: Matthew 11:4-5.
3. See: Mark 1:44.
4. Candy Gunther Brown, *Testing Prayer: Science and Healing* (Cambridge, MA: Harvard University Press, 2012), 7.
5. See: James 5:14.
6. See: www.cia.gov/library/publications/the-world -factbook/geos/mz.html.
7. See: www.pearsoneyecare.com/2013/06/30/ understanding-the-eye-chart.

Chapter 6

1. Doyle changes names of the people he talks about in the Middle East to protect their identity and keep them from potential danger.
2. See John 14:27.
3. Doyle tells a more complete story about Noor in: Tom Doyle with Greg Webster, *Dreams and Visions*, 3-12.
4. Tom Doyle with Greg Webster, *Dreams and Visions* (Nashville, TN: Thomas Nelson, 2012), 127.

Chapter 7

1. Based on a true story about a boy in Roger E. Olson's church, told during an interview with Lee Strobel for this book.
2. Story from "Lighthouse" section of *Focus on the Family Clubhouse* magazine, January 2018, p. 5.

Chapter 8

1. Tricia Lott Williford, "When Everyone Else is Getting Their Miracle: How to Deal with Feeling Overlooked," *Ann Voskamp* blog, July 10, 2017. www.annvoskamp.com/2017/07/when-everyone-else-is-getting-their-miracle-how-to-deal-with-feeling-overlooked.
2. See: Isaiah 55:8-9.
3. See: Matthew 13:53-58 and Mark 6:1-6.
4. See: Matthew 17:14-16.
5. See: 2 Timothy 4:20.
6. See my interview with philosopher Peter Kreeft of Boston College in *The Case for Faith*, 25-55.
7. See: Matthew 27:46 and Psalm 22:1.
8. See: Romans 5:3-5.
9. See: Matthew 26:36-42.
10. See: John 10:10.
11. See: Psalm 23:4.

Conclusion

1. Ephesians 2:8-9: "For it is by grace you have been saved, through faith—and this is not from yourselves, it is the gift of God—not by works, so that no one can boast."
2. Romans 3:23: "... For all have sinned and fall short of the glory of God." Romans 5:8: "But God demonstrates his own love for us in this: While we were sinners, Christ died for us." Romans 6:23: "For the wages of sin is death, but the gift of God is eternal life in Christ Jesus our Lord." Romans 10:9-10: "If you declare with your mouth, 'Jesus is Lord,' and believe in your heart that God raised him from the dead, you will be saved. For it is with your heart that you believe and are justified, and it is with your mouth that you profess your faith and are saved." Romans 10:13: "... Everyone who calls on the name of the Lord will be saved."
3. Proverbs 2:3-5.

Case for Christ
for Kids, Updated and
Expanded

Lee Strobel

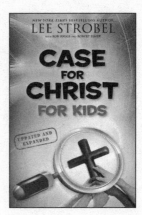

You meet skeptics every day. They ask questions like:

Was Jesus really born in a stable?

Did his friends tell the truth?

Did he really come back from the dead?

Here's a book written in kid-friendly language that gives you all the answers.

Packed full of well-researched, reliable, and eye-opening investigations of some of the biggest questions you have, *Case for Christ for Kids* brings Christ to life by addressing the existence, miracles, ministry, and resurrection of Jesus of Nazareth.

Pick up a copy at your favorite bookstore or online!

Case for Grace for Kids

Lee Strobel

What does "grace" really mean? How can God's grace impact your life? How can you experience grace every day?

This new book by *New York Times* best-selling author Lee Strobel shows how God's love is for everyone—no matter what. Through stories of everyday people whose lives have been changed, you will discover God's love and the power of forgiveness. You will experience God's amazing grace and be able to share it with others.